P9-CQL-890

GREAT JOBS

FOR

Political Science Majors

Mark Rowh

VGM Career Books

Chicago   New York   San Francisco   Lisbon   London   Madrid   Mexico City
Milan   New Delhi   San Juan   Seoul   Singapore   Sydney   Toronto

Library of Congress Cataloging-in-Publication Data

Rowh, Mark.
    Great jobs for political science majors / Mark Rowh. — 2nd ed.
        p.   cm. — (Great jobs for)
    Includes index.
    ISBN 0-07-141159-3
        1. Political science—Vocational guidance—United States.   2. College graduates—
Employment—United States.   3. Occupations—United States.   I. Title.   II. Series.

    JA88.U6R68   2003
    320'.023'73—dc21   2003050157

1 2 3 4 5 6 7 8 9 0   AGM/AGM   2 1 0 9 8 7 6 5 4 3

ISBN 0-07-141159-3

Series design by Jennifer Locke

McGraw-Hill books are available at special quantity discounts to use as premiums and sales promotions, or for use in corporate training programs. For more information, please write to the Director of Special Sales, Professional Publishing, McGraw-Hill, Two Penn Plaza, New York, NY 10121-2298. Or contact your local bookstore.

This book is printed on acid-free paper.

To David Rowh and all the young men and women who have served their country through the AmeriCorps program.

Contents

Acknowledgments

The author offers grateful thanks to the following for their cooperation in providing information for this book:

Alzheimer's Association
American Association for Employment in Education
American Bar Association
American Political Science Association
Canadian Political Science Association
Case Western Reserve University
Concordia College
Midwest Political Science Association
Rose Miskowiec
National Association of Law Placement
National Association of Schools of Public Affairs and Administration
National Education Association
Northwestern University
Radford University
Linda Rowh
The University of Calgary
The University of Minnesota
U.S. Department of Labor
Vanderbilt University
Virginia Department of Education
Washington University

Introduction

Political Science: Pathway to Success

Political science is one of the most popular areas of study for today's college students. Those who enroll in political science programs range from undergraduates who complete a major or minor in political science or a related area, to graduate students who earn a master's or doctoral degree in the field.

Political science is not just popular, however. It is also an important area of academic inquiry and career preparation. In studying political science, you've learned just how vital government and political institutions are to modern life. Without government and the political processes that support it, virtually any culture would dissolve into anarchy. Sure, government can be intrusive, inflexible, cumbersome, and expensive. But it also serves as the foundation for law, commerce, personal freedom, and other fundamental components of a civilized society. Of course, if you're a political science major, you already know about the importance of the political realm. What you may not realize is that those who study political science enjoy a wide range of career options.

Perhaps you chose a major in political science because you hope to attend law school, which is a perfectly valid reason. Many students use an undergraduate degree with a major in political science as the first step toward attending law school and becoming an attorney.

On the other hand, maybe you haven't really considered the law school option. If that is the case, don't overlook this opportunity. Law school isn't for everyone, and neither is a legal career. But as a political science major, you may want to examine this direction just to make sure your decision is based on facts rather than general impressions.

Or let's go in another direction. Perhaps you have thought about going into politics. If so, what academic preparation could serve you better than political science? Maybe someday you'll run for the state legislature, the U.S. Congress, the governorship of your state, or an even higher position. Who knows? Maybe a political science degree will help you win a ticket to Air Force One!

Then again, maybe you haven't considered a political career. Given your interest in government and the credentials a political science degree provides, you may want to explore this path. Or you may want to think about a government service career, where you work for the federal government or a state or local government agency.

Or how about teaching? Or journalism? Or business? The truth is, a political science background can lead in many different directions.

A Field with Few Limits

Does majoring in political science make you a political scientist? Actually, completing a major in this field doesn't lead to just one end result. Political science majors perform an impressively diverse range of jobs.

In its brochure "Political Science: An Ideal Liberal Arts Major," the American Political Science Association lists examples of the actual positions held by political science graduates. Just a few titles on this wide-ranging list are

- Adviser to chairman of state Energy Commission
- Campaign finance analyst
- Chief, state general government services office
- CIA, advanced concepts staff, Office of Research and Development
- Commissioner, state Department of Human Services
- County clerk
- Deputy secretary for administration, state Department of Welfare
- Executive director, special interest association
- Federal commission senior policy analyst
- International research specialist
- Labor relations specialist
- Library of Congress, specialist
- Plans and review officer, U.S. Information Agency
- Private foundation program director
- Public affairs research analyst
- Senior employee relations analyst
- Supervisor, state Department of Education

- Television network, director of surveys
- U.S. Army, strategic planning specialist
- U.S. consulate, principal officer

These are just some of the jobs held by political science grads. Those with political science backgrounds can flourish in government, law, business, education, and the nonprofit sector, among other areas.

The Ideal Political Science Graduate

The ideal political science graduate might be a specialist. He or she may have concentrated in a specific field of study such as international relations, preparing to perform a narrow range of duties. Or the ideal political science grad could be a generalist. Such a person may be prepared to take on almost any entry-level position. Armed with the analytical and communication skills of the liberal arts graduate, plus an understanding of government and how it works, the political science grad has much to offer. This is true both in the working world and in graduate studies.

So who is the ideal political science graduate? The ideal person is ready to seize the opportunities made possible by his or her studies in this field. Whether it means going on to advanced studies or entering the workforce, a major in political science can open many doors.

PART ONE

THE JOB SEARCH

The Self-Assessment

Self-assessment is the process by which you begin to acknowledge your own particular blend of education, experiences, values, needs, and goals. It provides the foundation for career planning and the entire job search process. Self-assessment involves looking inward and asking yourself what can sometimes prove to be difficult questions. This self-examination should lead to an intimate understanding of your personal traits, your personal values, your consumption patterns and economic needs, your longer-term goals, your skill base, your preferred skills, and your underdeveloped skills.

You come to the self-assessment process knowing yourself well in some of these areas, but you may still be uncertain about other aspects. You may be well aware of your consumption patterns, but have you spent much time specifically identifying your longer-term goals or your personal values as they relate to work? No matter what level of self-assessment you have undertaken to date, it is now time to clarify all of these issues and questions as they relate to the job search.

The knowledge you gain in the self-assessment process will guide the rest of your job search. In this book, you will learn about all of the following tasks:

- Writing résumés and cover letters
- Researching careers and networking
- Interviewing and job offer considerations

In each of these steps, you will rely on and often return to the understanding gained through your self-assessment. Any individual seeking employment must be able and willing to express these facets of his or her personality to recruiters and interviewers throughout the job search. This communication allows you to show the world who you are so that together with employers you can determine whether there will be a workable match with a given job or career path.

How to Conduct a Self-Assessment

The self-assessment process goes on naturally all the time. People ask you to clarify what you mean, you make a purchasing decision, or you begin a new relationship. You react to the world and the world reacts to you. How you understand these interactions and any changes you might make because of them are part of the natural process of self-discovery. There is, however, a more comprehensive and efficient way to approach self-assessment with regard to employment.

Because self-assessment can become a complex exercise, we have distilled it into a seven-step process that provides an effective basis for undertaking a job search. The seven steps include the following:

1. Understanding your personal traits
2. Identifying your personal values
3. Calculating your economic needs
4. Exploring your longer-term goals
5. Enumerating your skill base
6. Recognizing your preferred skills
7. Assessing skills needing further development

As you work through your self-assessment, you might want to create a worksheet similar to the one shown in Exhibit 1.1, starting on the following page. Or you might want to keep a journal of the thoughts you have as you undergo this process. There will be many opportunities to revise your self-assessment as you start down the path of seeking a career.

Step 1 Understand Your Personal Traits
Each person has a unique personality that he or she brings to the job search process. Gaining a better understanding of your personal traits can help you evaluate job and career choices. Identifying these traits and then finding employment that allows you to draw on at least some of them can create a

Exhibit 1.1
SELF-ASSESSMENT WORKSHEET

Step 1. Understand Your Personal Traits

The personal traits that describe me are:
(Include all of the words that describe you.)
The ten personal traits that most accurately describe me are:
(List these ten traits.)

Step 2. Identify Your Personal Values

Working conditions that are important to me include:
(List working conditions that would have to exist for you to accept a position.)
The values that go along with my working conditions are:
(Write down the values that correspond to each working condition.)
Some additional values I've decided to include are:
(List those values you identify as you conduct this job search.)

Step 3. Calculate Your Economic Needs

My estimated minimum annual salary requirement is:
(Write the salary you have calculated based on your budget.)
Starting salaries for the positions I'm considering are:
(List the name of each job you are considering and the associated starting salary.)

Step 4. Explore Your Longer-Term Goals

My thoughts on longer-term goals right now are:
(Jot down some of your longer-term goals as you know them right now.)

Step 5. Enumerate Your Skill Base

The general skills I possess are:
(List the skills that underlie tasks you are able to complete.)
The specific skills I possess are:
(List more technical or specific skills that you possess, and indicate your level of expertise.)
General and specific skills that I want to promote to employers for the jobs I'm considering are:
(List general and specific skills for each type of job you are considering.)

continued

Step 6. Recognize Your Preferred Skills

Skills that I would like to use on the job include:

(List skills that you hope to use on the job, and indicate how often you'd like to use them.)

Step 7. Assess Skills Needing Further Development

Some skills that I'll need to acquire for the jobs I'm considering include:

(Write down skills listed in job advertisements or job descriptions that you don't currently possess.)

I believe I can build these skills by:

(Describe how you plan to acquire these skills.)

---

rewarding and fulfilling work experience. If potential employment doesn't allow you to use these preferred traits, it is important to decide whether you can find other ways to express them or whether you would be better off not considering this type of job. Interests and hobbies pursued outside of work hours can be one way to use personal traits you don't have an opportunity to draw on in your work. For example, if you consider yourself an outgoing person and the kinds of jobs you are examining allow little contact with other people, you may be able to achieve the level of interaction that is comfortable for you outside of your work setting. If such a compromise seems impractical or otherwise unsatisfactory, you probably should explore only jobs that provide the interaction you want and need on the job.

Many young adults who are not very confident about their employability will downplay their need for income. They will say, "Money is not all that important if I love my work." But if you begin to document exactly what you need for housing, transportation, insurance, clothing, food, and utilities, you will begin to understand that some jobs cannot meet your financial needs and it doesn't matter how wonderful the job is. If you have to worry each payday about bills and other financial obligations, you won't be very effective on the job. Begin now to be honest with yourself about your needs.

Begin the self-assessment process by creating an inventory of your personal traits. Make a list of as many words as possible to describe yourself. Words like *accurate, creative, future-oriented, relaxed,* or *structured* are just a few examples. In addition, you might ask people who know you well how they might describe you.

Focus on Selected Personal Traits. Of all the traits you identified, select the ten you believe most accurately describe you. Keep track of these ten traits.

Consider Your Personal Traits in the Job Search Process. As you begin exploring jobs and careers, watch for matches between your personal traits and the job descriptions you read. Some jobs will require many personal traits you know you possess, and others will not seem to match those traits.

Working as a legislative assistant, for example, will draw upon your organizational, analytical, and communicative skills. You will need to gather and analyze information from a variety of sources, and then summarize or explain important details. Such activity may range from listening to a constituent's complaints and drafting a letter in response, to studying proposed legislation and recommending whether your employer should support it. You may not need a legislator's level of public-speaking abilities, but your job will demand attention to detail and a good memory.

Your ability to respond to changing conditions, your decision-making ability, productivity, creativity, and verbal skills all have a bearing on your success in and enjoyment of your work life. To better guarantee success, be sure to take the time needed to understand these traits in yourself.

Step 2   Identify Your Personal Values

Your personal values affect every aspect of your life, including employment, and they develop and change as you move through life. Values can be defined as principles that we hold in high regard, qualities that are important and desirable to us. Some values aren't ordinarily connected to work (love, beauty, color, light, relationships, family, or religion), and others are (autonomy, cooperation, effectiveness, achievement, knowledge, and security). Our values determine, in part, the level of satisfaction we feel in a particular job.

Define Acceptable Working Conditions. One facet of employment is the set of working conditions that must exist for someone to consider taking a job.

Each of us would probably create a unique list of acceptable working conditions, but items that might be included on many people's lists are the amount of money you would need to be paid, how far you are willing to drive or travel, the amount of freedom you want in determining your own schedule, whether you would be working with people or data or things, and the types of tasks you would be willing to do. Your conditions might include statements of working conditions you will *not* accept; for example, you might not be willing to work at night or on weekends or holidays.

If you were offered a job tomorrow, what conditions would have to exist for you to realistically consider accepting the position? Take some time and make a list of these conditions.

Realize Associated Values. Your list of working conditions can be used to create an inventory of your values relating to jobs and careers you are exploring. For example, if one of your conditions stated that you wanted to earn at least $30,000 per year, the associated value would be financial gain. If another condition was that you wanted to work with a friendly group of people, the value that went along with that might be belonging or interaction with people.

Relate Your Values to the World of Work. As you read the job descriptions you come across either in this book, in newspapers and magazines, or online, think about the values associated with each position.

For example, when working as a legislative assistant, your duties may include writing draft versions of speeches or reports, scheduling meetings for your employer, and talking on the telephone with constituents or potential voters.

At least some of the associated values in the field you're exploring should match those you extracted from your list of working conditions. Take a second look at any values that don't match up. How important are they to you? What will happen if they are not satisfied on the job? Can you incorporate those personal values elsewhere? Your answers need to be brutally honest. As you continue your exploration, be sure to add to your list any additional values that occur to you.

Step 3   Calculate Your Economic Needs

Each of us grew up in an environment that provided for certain basic needs, such as food and shelter, and, to varying degrees, other needs that we now consider basic, such as cable television, E-mail, or an automobile. Needs such as privacy, space, and quiet, which at first glance may not appear to be monetary needs, may add to housing expenses and so should be considered as you examine your economic needs. For example, if you place a high value on a large, open living space for yourself, it would be difficult to satisfy that need without an associated high housing cost, especially in a densely populated city environment.

As you prepare to move into the world of work and become responsible for meeting your own basic needs, it is important to consider the salary you will need to be able to afford a satisfying standard of living. The three-step process outlined here will help you plan a budget, which in turn will allow you to evaluate the various career choices and geographic locations you are considering. The steps include (1) developing a realistic budget, (2) examining starting salaries, and (3) using a cost-of-living index.

Develop a Realistic Budget. Each of us has certain expectations for the kind of lifestyle we want to maintain. To begin the process of defining your economic needs, it will be helpful to determine what you expect to spend on routine monthly expenses. These expenses include housing, food, transportation, entertainment, utilities, loan repayments, and revolving charge accounts. You may not currently spend anything for certain items, but you probably will have to once you begin supporting yourself. As you develop this budget, be generous in your estimates, but keep in mind any items that could be reduced or eliminated. If you are not sure about the cost of a certain item, talk with family or friends who would be able to give you a realistic estimate.

If this is new or difficult for you, start to keep a log of expenses right now. You may be surprised at how much you actually spend each month for food or stamps or magazines. Household expenses and personal grooming items can often loom very large in a budget, as can auto repairs or home maintenance.

Income taxes must also be taken into consideration when examining salary requirements. State and local taxes vary, so it is difficult to calculate exactly the effect of taxes on the amount of income you need to generate. To roughly estimate the gross income necessary to generate your minimum annual salary requirement, multiply the minimum salary you have calculated by a factor of 1.35. The resulting figure will be an approximation of what your gross income would need to be, given your estimated expenses.

Examine Starting Salaries. Starting salaries for each of the career tracks are provided throughout this book. These salary figures can be used in conjunction with the cost-of-living index (discussed in the next section) to determine whether you would be able to meet your basic economic needs in a given geographic location.

Use a Cost-of-Living Index. If you are thinking about trying to get a job in a geographic region other than the one where you now live, understanding differences in the cost of living will help you come to a more informed decision about making a move. By using a cost-of-living index, you can compare salaries offered and the cost of living in different locations with what you know about the salaries offered and the cost of living in your present location.

Many variables are used to calculate the cost-of-living index. Often included are housing, groceries, utilities, transportation, health care, clothing, and entertainment expenses. Right now you do not need to worry about the details associated with calculating a given index. The main purpose of this exercise is to help you understand that pay ranges for entry-level positions may not vary greatly, but the cost of living in different locations *can* vary tremendously.

Say you lived in Cleveland, Ohio, for example, and found that the average salary for a high school political science teacher was $40,000 annually. Now, however, you're thinking about moving to New York, Los Angeles, or Denver. You know you can live on $40,000 in Cleveland, but you want to be able to equal that salary in other locations you're considering. How much will you need to earn in those locations to do this? Figuring the cost of living for each city will show you.

Let's walk through this example. In any cost-of-living index, the number 100 represents the national average cost of living, and each city is assigned an index number based on current prices in that city for the items included in the index (housing, food, etc.). In the index we used, New York was assigned the number 213.3, Los Angeles's index was 124.6, Denver's was 100.0, and Cleveland's index was 114.3. In other words, it costs more than twice as much to live in New York as it does in Denver. We can set up a table to determine exactly how much you would have to earn in each of these cities to have the same buying power that you have in Cleveland. You would have to earn $74,646 in New York,

City	Index	Equivalent Salary
New York	213.3 /	× $40,000 = $74,646 in New York
Cleveland	114.3	
Los Angeles	124.6 /	× $40,000 = $43,604 in Los Angeles
Cleveland	114.3	
Denver	100.0 /	× $40,000 = $34,996 in Denver
Cleveland	114.3	

$43,604 in Los Angeles, and $34,996 in Denver to match the buying power of $40,000 in Cleveland.

If you would like to determine whether it's financially worthwhile to make any of these moves, one more piece of information is needed: the salaries of high school political science teachers in these other cities. One source of such information is *The American Salaries and Wages Survey*, published by Gale, a division of the Thompson Corporation (galegroup .com). This publication incorporated salary data from more than 300 data sources, covering more than 4,400 occupations. Other sources of salary information include the human resources offices of school districts in cities you are considering.

Once you obtain a salary estimate in a given city, you can include it in your calculations along with general differences in the cost of living. By combining the two factors, you can determine whether you would increase or decrease your buying power when moving to another city.

You can work through a similar exercise for any type of job you are considering and for many locations when current salary information is available. It will be worth your time to undertake this analysis if you are seriously considering a relocation. By doing so you will be able to make an informed choice.

Step 4 Explore Your Longer-Term Goals

There is no question that when we first begin working, our goals are to use our skills and education in a job that will reward us with employment, income, and status relative to the preparation we brought with us to this position. If we are not being paid as much as we feel we should for our level of education or if job demands don't provide the intellectual stimulation we had hoped for, we experience unhappiness and as a result often seek other employment.

Most jobs we consider "good" are those that fulfill our basic "lower-level" needs of security, food, clothing, shelter, income, and productive work. But even when our basic needs are met and our jobs are secure and productive, we as individuals are constantly changing. As we change, the demands and expectations we place on our jobs may change. Fortunately, some jobs grow and change with us, and this explains why some people are happy throughout many years in a job.

But more often people are bigger than the jobs they fill. We have more goals and needs than any job could satisfy. These are "higher-level" needs of self-esteem, companionship, affection, and an increasing desire to feel we are employing ourselves in the most effective way possible. Not all of these higher-level needs can be met through employment, but for as long as we are employed, we increasingly demand that our jobs play their part in moving us along the path to fulfillment.

Another obvious but important fact is that we change as we mature. Although our jobs also have the potential for change, they may not change as frequently or as markedly as we do. There are increasingly fewer one-job, one-employer careers; we must think about a work future that may involve voluntary or forced moves from employer to employer. Because of that very real possibility, we need to take advantage of the opportunities in each position we hold. Acquiring the skills and competencies associated with each position will keep us viable and attractive as employees. This is particularly true in a job market that not only is technology/computer dependent, but also is populated with more and more small, self-transforming organizations rather than the large, seemingly stable organizations of the past.

If you are considering a position as an urban planner, you would gain a better perspective on this career by talking to an entry-level planning assistant, a more senior and experienced town planner or city planner, and finally, a director of planning for a city, town, or county who has had a considerable work history in urban planning. Each will have a difference perspective, unique concerns, and an individual set of value priorities.

Step 5   Enumerate Your Skill Base

In terms of the job search, skills can be thought of as capabilities that can be developed in school, at work, or by volunteering and then used in specific job settings. Many studies have documented the kinds of skills that employers seek in entry-level applicants. For example, some of the most desired skills for individuals interested in the teaching profession are the ability to interact effectively with students one-on-one, to manage a classroom, to adapt to varying situations as necessary, and to get involved in school activities. Business employers have also identified important qualities, including enthusiasm for the employer's product or service, a businesslike mind, the ability to follow written or oral instructions, the ability to demonstrate self-control, the confidence to suggest new ideas, the ability to communicate with all members of a group, an awareness of cultural differences, and loyalty, to name just a few. You will find that many of these skills are also in the repertoire of qualities demanded in your college major.

To be successful in obtaining any given job, you must be able to demonstrate that you possess a certain mix of skills that will allow you to carry out the duties required by that job. This skill mix will vary a great deal from job to job; to determine the skills necessary for the jobs you are seeking, you can read job advertisements or more generic job descriptions, such as those found later in this book. If you want to be effective in the job search, you must directly show employers that you possess the skills needed to be successful in filling the position. These skills will initially be described on your résumé and then discussed again during the interview process.

Skills are either general or specific. To develop a list of skills relevant to employers, you must first identify the general skills you possess, then list specific skills you have to offer, and, finally, examine which of these skills employers are seeking.

Identify Your General Skills. Because you possess or will possess a college degree, employers will assume that you can read and write, perform certain basic computations, think critically, and communicate effectively. Employers will want to see that you have acquired these skills, and they will want to know which additional general skills you possess.

One way to begin identifying skills is to write an experiential diary. An experiential diary lists all the tasks you were responsible for completing for each job you've held and then outlines the skills required to do those tasks. You may list several skills for any given task. This diary allows you to distinguish between the tasks you performed and the underlying skills required to complete those tasks. Here's an example:

Tasks	Skills
Answering telephone	Effective use of language, clear diction, ability to direct inquiries, ability to solve problems
Waiting on tables	Poise under conditions of time and pressure, speed, accuracy, good memory, simultaneous completion of tasks, sales skills

For each job or experience you have participated in, develop a worksheet based on the example shown here. On a résumé, you may want to describe these skills rather than simply listing tasks. Skills are easier for the employer to appreciate, especially when your experience is very different from the employment you are seeking. In addition to helping you identify general skills, this experiential diary will prepare you to speak more effectively in an interview about the qualifications you possess.

Identify Your Specific Skills. It may be easier to identify your specific skills because you can definitely say whether you can speak other languages, program a computer, draft a map or diagram, or edit a document using appropriate symbols and terminology.

Using your experiential diary, identify the points in your history where you learned how to do something very specific, and decide whether you have a beginning, intermediate, or advanced knowledge of how to use that particular skill. Right now, be sure to list *every* specific skill you have, and don't consider whether you like using the skill. Write down a list of specific skills you have acquired and the level of competence you possess—beginning, intermediate, or advanced.

Relate Your Skills to Employers. You probably have thought about a couple of different jobs you might be interested in obtaining, and one way to begin relating the general and specific skills you possess to a potential employer's needs is to read actual advertisements for these types of positions (see Part Two for resources listing actual job openings).

For example, you might be interested in working as an economic analyst for a government agency that deals with foreign trade, before returning to graduate school to seek a master's degree in international relations with a specialty in economics. A typical job listing might read "conduct trade policy analysis, economic evaluations, and import-export studies. Bachelor's degree in economics, international business, or political science required. International experience preferred." If you then used one of the general sources of information that describe the job of a policy analyst or international trade specialist, you would find additional information. Policy analysts in this area track and report on trade laws and policies, interpret laws and regulations, and advise senior managers about economic and political policies.

Begin building a comprehensive list of required skills with the first job description you read. Exploring advertisements for several types of related positions will reveal an important core of skills necessary for obtaining the type of work you're interested in. Include both general and specific skills.

The following is a sample list of skills needed to be successful as a policy analyst in international trade.

General Skills	Specific Skills
Accounting	Estimating trade volume
Reading	Tracking development of
Gathering information	foreign legislation related
Decision making	to trade
Meeting deadlines	Compiling trade figures
Attending meetings	Evaluating alternatives
Entering data into	Preparing reports
computer	Communicating
Writing	recommendations for
	policy changes
	Preparing quarterly trade
	summaries
	Editing trade reports

On a separate sheet of paper, try to generate a list of required skills for at least one job you are considering. The list of general skills that you develop for a given career path would be valuable for any number of jobs you may seek. Many specific skills would also be transferable to other types of positions. For example, editing reports is a required skill for other types of analysts and for almost any management position. The ability to use basic word processing and spreadsheet software would also be useful in almost any job setting.

Step 6 Recognize Your Preferred Skills

In the previous section you developed a comprehensive list of skills that relate to particular career paths that are of interest to you. You can now relate these to skills that you prefer to use. We all use a wide range of skills (some researchers say individuals have a repertoire of about five hundred skills), but we may not particularly be interested in using all of them in our work. There may be some skills that come to us more naturally or that we use successfully time and time again and that we want to continue to use; these are best described as our preferred skills. For this exercise use the list of skills that you created for the previous section, and decide which of them you are *most interested in using* in future work and how often you would like to use them. You might be interested in using some skills only occasionally, while others you would like to use more regularly. You probably also have skills that you hope you can use constantly.

As you examine job announcements, look for matches between this list of preferred skills and the qualifications described in the advertisements. These skills should be highlighted on your résumé and discussed in job interviews.

Step 7 Assess Skills Needing Further Development

Previously you compiled a list of general and specific skills required for given positions. You already possess some of these skills; those that remain to be developed are your underdeveloped skills.

If you are just beginning the job search, there may be gaps between the qualifications required for some of the jobs you're considering and the skills you possess. The thought of having to admit to and talk about these underdeveloped skills, especially in a job interview, is a frightening one. One way to put a healthy perspective on this subject is to target and relate your exploration of underdeveloped skills to the types of positions you are seeking. Recognizing these shortcomings and planning to overcome them with either on-the-job training or additional formal education can be a positive way to address the concept of underdeveloped skills.

On your worksheet or in your journal, make a list of up to five general or specific skills required for the positions you're interested in that you *don't currently possess*. For each item list an idea you have for specific action you could take to acquire that skill. Do some brainstorming to come up with possible actions. If you have a hard time generating ideas, talk to people currently working in this type of position, professionals in your college career services office, trusted friends, family members, or members of related professional associations.

In the chapter on interviewing, we will discuss in detail how to effectively address questions about underdeveloped skills. Generally speaking, though, employers want genuine answers to these types of questions. They want you to reveal "the real you," and they also want to see how you answer difficult questions. In taking the positive, targeted approach discussed previously, you show the employer that you are willing to continue to learn and that you have a plan for strengthening your job qualifications.

Use Your Self-Assessment

Exploring entry-level career options can be an exciting experience if you have good resources available and will take the time to use them. Can you effectively complete the following tasks?

1. Understand your personality traits and relate them to career choices
2. Define your personal values
3. Determine your economic needs
4. Explore longer-term goals
5. Understand your skill base
6. Recognize your preferred skills
7. Express a willingness to improve on your underdeveloped skills

If so, then you can more meaningfully participate in the job search process by writing a more effective résumé, finding job titles that represent work you are interested in doing, locating job sites that will provide the opportunity for you to use your strengths and skills, networking in an informed way, participating in focused interviews, getting the most out of follow-up contacts, and evaluating job offers to find those that create a good match between you and the employer. The remaining chapters in Part One guide you through these next steps in the job search process. For many job seekers, this process can take anywhere from three months to a year to implement. The time you will need to put into your job search will depend on the type of job you want and the geographic location where you'd like to work. Think of your effort as a job in itself, requiring you to set aside time each week to complete the needed work. Carefully undertaken efforts may reduce the time you need for your job search.

2

The Résumé and Cover Letter

The task of writing a résumé may seem overwhelming if you are unfamiliar with this type of document, but there are some easily understood techniques that can and should be used. This section was written to help you understand the purpose of the résumé, the different types of résumé formats available, and how to write the sections of information traditionally found on a résumé. We will present examples and explanations that address questions frequently posed by people writing their first résumé or updating an old résumé.

Even within the formats and suggestions given, however, there are infinite variations. True, most résumés follow one of the outlines suggested, but you should feel free to adjust the résumé to suit your needs and make it expressive of your life and experience.

Why Write a Résumé?

The purpose of a résumé is to convince an employer that you should be interviewed. Whether you're mailing, faxing, or E-mailing this document, you'll want to present enough information to show that you can make an immediate and valuable contribution to an organization. A résumé is not an indepth historical or legal document; later in the job search process you may be asked to document your entire work history on an application form and attest to its validity. The résumé should, instead, highlight relevant information pertaining directly to the organization that will receive the document or to the type of position you are seeking.

We will discuss the chronological and digital résumés in detail here. Functional and targeted résumés, which are used much less often, are briefly discussed. The reasons for using one type of résumé over another and the typical format for each are addressed in the following sections.

The Chronological Résumé

The chronological résumé is the most common of the various résumé formats and therefore the format that employers are most used to receiving. This type of résumé is easy to read and understand because it details the chronological progression of jobs you have held. (See Exhibit 2.1.) It begins with your most recent employment and works back in time. If you have a solid work history or have experience that provided growth and development in your duties and responsibilities, a chronological résumé will highlight these achievements. The typical elements of a chronological résumé include the heading, a career objective, educational background, employment experience, activities, and references.

The Heading
The heading consists of your name, address, telephone number, and other means of contact. This may include a fax number, E-mail address, and your home-page address. If you are using a shared E-mail account or a parent's business fax, be sure to let others who use these systems know that you may receive important professional correspondence via these systems. You wouldn't want to miss a vital E-mail or fax! Likewise, if your résumé directs readers to a personal home page on the Web, be certain it's a professional personal home page designed to be viewed and appreciated by a prospective employer. This may mean making substantial changes in the home page you currently mount on the Web.

The Objective
Without a doubt the objective statement is the most challenging part of the résumé for most writers. Even for individuals who have decided on a career path, it can be difficult to encapsulate all they want to say in one or two brief sentences. For job seekers who are unfocused or unclear about their intentions, trying to write this section can inhibit the entire résumé writing process.

Keep the objective as short as possible and no longer than two short sentences.

Exhibit 2.1
CHRONOLOGICAL RÉSUMÉ

JENNY VAN HORN

Apartment 234
Appleton Way Village
Marietta, GA 30061
(770) 555-1858
jennyvh@xxx.net

OBJECTIVE
Position teaching Civics or American Government in a high school or middle school setting.

EDUCATION
Bachelor of Science, University of Georgia
Athens, Georgia, May 2003
Major: Political Education
Minor: Teacher Education

Honors/Activities:
Vice President of Student Government Association
President, Political Science Club
Member, Student Ambassadors
Dean's List four semesters, President's List three semesters
Recipient, John Waggens Award (outstanding political science student)
Magna cum laude graduate

EXPERIENCE
Peer Tutor, University of Georgia Academic Support Center, 2001–2002
Provided tutoring in a variety of subjects for freshmen experiencing academic
    difficulty
Youth Counselor, Trinity United Methodist Church, Dublin, Georgia, 2001–2003
Assisted youth minister in planning youth activities, conducting weekly sessions,
    and providing oversight during retreats and other activities.
Intern, Georgia Political Action Center, Summer 1998
Assisted in compiling election data and completing reports regarding voter
    preferences in 1998 elections

continued

COMMUNITY SERVICE

Active volunteer with church activities; election day poll worker; Habitat for Humanity volunteer

REFERENCES

A selection of both personal and professional references will be provided on request.

Choose one of the following types of objective statement:

1. General Objective Statement

- An entry-level educational programming coordinator position

2. Position-Focused Objective

- To obtain the position of conference coordinator at State College

3. Industry-Focused Objective

- To begin a career as a sales representative in the cruise line industry

4. Summary of Qualifications Statement

A degree in political science and four years of progressively increasing job responsibility in a regional planning agency have prepared me to begin a career as a manager in a government agency that values thoroughness and attention to detail.

Support Your Objective. A résumé that contains any one of these types of objective statements should then go on to demonstrate why you are qualified to get the position. Listing academic degrees can be one way to indicate qualifications. Another demonstration would be in the way previous experiences, both volunteer and paid, are described. Without this kind of documentation in the body of the résumé, the objective looks unsupported. Think of the résumé as telling a connected story about you. All the elements should work together to form a coherent picture that ideally should relate to your statement of objective.

Education

This section of your résumé should indicate the exact name of the degree you will receive or have received, spelled out completely with no abbreviations. The degree is generally listed after the objective, followed by the institution name and location, and then the month and year of graduation. This section could also include your academic minor, grade point average (GPA), and appearance on the Dean's List or President's List.

If you have enough space, you might want to include a section listing courses related to the field in which you are seeking work. The best use of a "related courses" section would be to list some course work that is not traditionally associated with the major. Perhaps you took several computer courses outside your degree that will be helpful and related to the job prospects you are entertaining. Several education section examples are shown here:

- Bachelor of Science degree in Political Science
  State University, Boulder, Colorado, 2003
  Concentration: American Government Systems
- Bachelor of Science degree with major in Political
  Science
  University of South Carolina, Columbia, SC, May 2003
  Minor: U.S. History
- Bachelor of Arts degree in Political Science
  West Virginia State College, Institute, West Virginia,
  2003
  General Political Science option
  Minor in History

An example of a format for related-courses section follows:

RELATED COURSES	
American Government	Judicial Systems
Constitutional Law	Legislative Processes
State and Local Government	Advanced Seminar: The Electoral Process

---

Experience

The experience section of your résumé should be the most substantial part and should take up most of the space on the page. Employers want to see what kind of work history you have. They will look at your range of experiences, longevity in jobs, and specific tasks you are able to complete. This section may also be called "work experience," "related experience," "employment history," or "employment." No matter what you call this section, some important points to remember are the following:

1. **Describe your duties** as they relate to the position you are seeking.
2. **Emphasize major responsibilities** and indicate increases in responsibility. Include all relevant employment experiences: summer, part-time, internships, cooperative education, or self-employment.
3. **Emphasize skills**, especially those that transfer from one situation to another. The fact that you coordinated a student organization, chaired meetings, supervised others, and managed a budget leads one to suspect that you could coordinate other things as well.
4. **Use descriptive job titles** that provide information about what you did. A "Student Intern" should be more specifically stated as, for example, "Magazine Operations Intern." "Volunteer" is also too general; a title such as "Peer Writing Tutor" would be more appropriate.
5. **Create word pictures** by using active verbs to start sentences. Describe *results* you have produced in the work you have done.

A limp description would say something such as the following: "My duties included helping with production, proofreading, and editing. I used a design and page layout program." An action statement would be stated as follows: "Coordinated and assisted in the creative marketing of brochures and seminar promotions, becoming proficient in Quark."

Remember, an accomplishment is simply a result, a final measurable product that people can relate to. A duty is not a result; it is an obligation—every job holder has duties. For an effective résumé, list as many results as you can. To make the most of the limited space you have and to give your description impact, carefully select appropriate and accurate descriptors.

Here are some traits that employers tell us they like to see:

- Teamwork
- Energy and motivation

- Learning and using new skills
- Versatility
- Critical thinking
- Understanding how profits are created
- Organizational acumen
- Communicating directly and clearly, in both writing and speaking
- Risk taking
- Willingness to admit mistakes
- High personal standards

Solutions to Frequently Encountered Problems

Repetitive Employment with the Same Employer

EMPLOYMENT: The Foot Locker, Portland, Oregon. Summer 2001, 2002, 2003. Initially employed in high school as salesclerk. Due to successful performance, asked to return next two summers at higher pay with added responsibility. Ranked as the #2 salesperson the first summer and #1 the next two summers. Assisted in arranging eye-catching retail displays; served as manager of other summer workers during owner's absence.

A Large Number of Jobs

EMPLOYMENT: Recent Hospitality Industry Experience: Affiliated with four upscale hotel/restaurant complexes (September 2001–February 2004), where I worked part- and full-time as a waiter, bartender, disc jockey, and bookkeeper to produce income for college.

Several Positions with the Same Employer

EMPLOYMENT: Coca-Cola Bottling Co., Burlington, Vermont, 2001–2004. In four years, I received three promotions, each with increased pay and responsibility.

Summer Sales Coordinator: Promoted to hire, train, and direct efforts of add-on staff of fifteen college-age route salespeople hired to meet summer peak demand for product.

Sales Administrator: Promoted to run home office sales desk, managing accounts and associated delivery schedules for professional sales force of ten people. Intensive phone work, daily interaction with all personnel, and strong knowledge of product line required.

Route Salesperson: Summer employment to travel and tourism industry sites that use Coke products. Met specific schedule demands, used good communication skills with wide variety of customers, and demonstrated strong selling skills. Named salesperson of the month for July and August of that year.

Questions Résumé Writers Often Ask

How Far Back Should I Go in Terms of Listing Past Jobs?

Usually, listing three or four jobs should suffice. If you did something back in high school that has a bearing on your future aspirations for employment, by all means list the job. As you progress through your college career, high school jobs will be replaced on the résumé by college employment.

Should I Differentiate Between Paid and Nonpaid Employment?

Most employers are not initially concerned about how much you were paid. They are anxious to know how much responsibility you held in your past employment. There is no need to specify that your work was as a volunteer if you had significant responsibilities.

How Should I Represent My Accomplishments or Work-Related Responsibilities?

Succinctly, but fully. In other words, give the employer enough information to arouse curiosity but not so much detail that you leave nothing to the imagination. Besides, some jobs merit more lengthy explanations than others. Be sure to convey any information that can give an employer a better understanding of the depth of your involvement at work. Did you supervise others? How many? Did your efforts result in a more efficient operation? How much did you increase efficiency? Did you handle a budget? How much? Were you promoted in a short time? Did you work two jobs at once or fifteen hours per week after high school? Where appropriate, quantify.

Should the Work Section Always Follow the Education Section on the Résumé?

Always lead with your strengths. If your education closely relates to the employment you now seek, put this section after the objective. If your education does not closely relate but you have a surplus of good work experiences, consider reversing the order of your sections to lead with employment, followed by education.

How Should I Present My Activities, Honors, Awards, Professional Societies, and Affiliations?

This section of the résumé can add valuable information for an employer to consider if used correctly. The rule of thumb for information in this section is to include only those activities that are in some way relevant to the objective stated on your résumé. If you can draw a valid connection between your activities and your objective, include them; if not, leave them out.

Professional affiliations and honors should all be listed; especially important are those related to your job objective. Social clubs and activities need not be a part of your résumé unless you hold a significant office or you are looking for a position related to your membership. Be aware that most prospective employers' principal concerns are related to your employability, not your social life. If you have any, publications can be included as an addendum to your résumé.

How Should I Handle References?

The use of references is considered a part of the interview process, and they should never be listed on a résumé. You would always provide references to a potential employer if requested to, so it is not even necessary to include this section on the résumé if space does not permit. If space is available, it is acceptable to include the following statement:

- REFERENCES: Furnished upon request.

The Functional Résumé

The functional résumé departs from a chronological résumé in that it organizes information by specific accomplishments in various settings: previous jobs, volunteer work, associations, and so forth. This type of résumé permits you to stress the substance of your experiences rather than the position titles you have held. You should consider using a functional résumé if you have held a series of similar jobs that relied on the same skills or abilities. There are many good books in which you can find examples of functional résumés, including *How to Write a Winning Resume* or *Resumes Made Easy*.

The Targeted Résumé

The targeted résumé focuses on specific work-related capabilities you can bring to a given position within an organization. Past achievements are listed to highlight your capabilities and the work history section is abbreviated.

Digital Résumés

Today's employers have to manage an enormous number of résumés. One of the most frequent complaints the writers of this series hear from students is the failure of employers to even acknowledge the receipt of a résumé and cover letter. Frequently, the reason for this poor response or nonresponse is the volume of applications received for every job. In an attempt to better manage the considerable labor investment involved in processing large numbers of résumés, many employers are requiring digital submission of résumés. There are two types of digital résumés: those that can be E-mailed or posted to a website, called *electronic résumés,* and those that can be "read" by a computer, commonly called *scannable résumés.* Though the format may be a bit different from the traditional "paper" résumé, the goal of both types of digital résumés is the same—to get you an interview! These résumés must be designed to be "technologically friendly." What that basically means to you is that they should be free of graphics and fancy formatting. (See Exhibit 2.2.)

Electronic Résumés

Sometimes referred to as plain-text résumés, electronic résumés are designed to be E-mailed to an employer or posted to one of many commercial Internet databases such as careerbuilder.com, America's Job Bank (ajb.dni.us), or Monster.com.

Some technical considerations:

- Electronic résumés must be written in American Standard Code for Information Interchange (ASCII), which is simply a plain-text format. These characters are universally recognized so that every computer can accurately read and understand them. To create an ASCII file of your current résumé, open your document, then save it as a text or ASCII file. This will eliminate all formatting. Edit as needed using your computer's text editor application.
- Use a standard-width typeface. Courier is a good choice because it is the font associated with ASCII in most systems.

Exhibit 2.2
DIGITAL RÉSUMÉ

CYNTHIA PORTER
265 Weston St.
Columbus, OH 43229
Phone : 614-555-8430
E-mail: cyporter@xxx.com

Put your name at the top on its own line.

Put your phone number on its own line.

KEYWORD SUMMARY
B.A. Political Science
Nonprofit management

Keywords make your résumé easier to find in a database.

Use a standard-width typeface.

WORK EXPERIENCE
Cleveland Community Foundation
Intern
Summer 2002
* Assisted in assembling grant proposals for review
by foundation staff. Provided general office support.

Use a space between asterisk and text.

No line should exceed sixty-five characters.

Dept. of Political Science
Case Western Reserve University
Student Assistant
2000-2002
* Assisted department chairperson in general office
duties. Conducted background research for grant-funded
project on voting practices in 19th-century America.

End each line by hitting the ENTER (or RETURN) key.

EDUCATION
Bachelor of Arts, Political Science, 2002
Case Western Reserve University, Cleveland, OH

Capitalize letters to emphasize headings.

- Use a font size of 11 to 14 points. A 12-point font is considered standard.
- Your margin should be left-justified.
- Do not exceed sixty-five characters per line because the word-wrap function doesn't operate in ASCII.
- Do not use boldface, italics, underlining, bullets, or various font sizes. Instead, use asterisks, plus signs, or all capital letters when you want to emphasize something.
- Avoid graphics and shading.
- Use as many "keywords" as you possibly can. These are words or phrases usually relating to skills or experience that either are specifically used in the job announcement or are popular buzzwords in the industry.
- Minimize abbreviations.
- Your name should be the first line of text.
- Conduct a "test run" by E-mailing your résumé to yourself and a friend before you send it to the employer. See how it transmits, and make any changes you need to. Continue to test it until it's exactly how you want it to look.
- Unless an employer specifically requests that you send the résumé in the form of an attachment, don't. Employers can encounter problems opening a document as an attachment, and there are always viruses to consider.
- Don't forget your cover letter. Send it along with your résumé as a single message.

Scannable Résumés

Some companies are relying on technology to narrow the candidate pool for available job openings. Electronic Applicant Tracking uses imaging to scan, sort, and store résumé elements in a database. Then, through OCR (Optical Character Recognition) software, the computer scans the résumés for key-words and phrases. To have the best chance at getting an interview, you want to increase the number of "hits"—matches of your skills, abilities, experience, and education to those the computer is scanning for—your résumé will get. You can see how critical using the right keywords is for this type of résumé.

Technical considerations include:

- Again, do not use boldface (newer systems may read this OK, but many older ones won't), italics, underlining, bullets, shading, graphics, or multiple font sizes. Instead, for emphasis, use asterisks, plus signs, or all capital letters. Minimize abbreviations.

- Use a popular typeface such as Courier, Helvetica, Ariel, or Palatino. Avoid decorative fonts.
- Font size should be between 11 and 14 points.
- Do not compress the spacing between letters.
- Use horizontal and vertical lines sparingly; the computer may misread them as the letters *L* or *I*.
- Left-justify the text.
- Do not use parentheses or brackets around telephone numbers, and be sure your phone number is on its own line of text.
- Your name should be the first line of text and on its own line. If your résumé is longer than one page, be sure to put your name on the top of all pages.
- Use a traditional résumé structure. The chronological format may work best.
- Use nouns that are skill-focused, such as *management, writer,* and *programming.* This is different from traditional paper résumés, which use action-oriented verbs.
- Laser printers produce the finest copies. Avoid dot-matrix printers.
- Use standard, light-colored paper with text on one side only. Since the higher the contrast, the better, your best choice is black ink on white paper.
- Always send original copies. If you must fax, set the fax on fine mode, not standard.
- Do not staple or fold your résumé. This can confuse the computer.
- Before you send your scannable résumé, be certain the employer uses this technology. If you can't determine this, you may want to send two versions (scannable and traditional) to be sure your résumé gets considered.

Résumé Production and Other Tips

An ink-jet printer is the preferred option for printing your résumé. Begin by printing just a few copies. You may find a small error or you may simply want to make some changes, and it is less frustrating and less expensive if you print in small batches.

Résumé paper color should be carefully chosen. You should consider the types of employers who will receive your résumé and the types of positions for which you are applying. Use white or ivory paper for traditional or conservative employers or for higher-level positions.

Black ink on sharp, white paper can be harsh on the reader's eyes. Think about an ivory or cream paper that will provide less contrast and be easier to read. Pink, green, and blue tints should generally be avoided.

Many résumé writers buy packages of matching envelopes and cover sheet stationery that, although not absolutely necessary, help convey a professional impression.

If you'll be producing many cover letters at home, be sure you have high-quality printing equipment. Learn standard envelope formats for business, and retain a copy of every cover letter you send out. You can use the copies to take notes of any telephone conversations that may occur.

If attending a job fair, either carry a briefcase or place your résumé in a nicely covered legal-size pad holder.

The Cover Letter

The cover letter provides you with the opportunity to tailor your résumé by telling the prospective employer how you can be a benefit to the organization. It allows you to highlight aspects of your background that are not already discussed in your résumé and that might be especially relevant to the organization you are contacting or to the position you are seeking. Every résumé should have a cover letter enclosed when you send it out. Unlike the résumé, which may be mass-produced, a cover letter is most effective when it is individually prepared and focused on the particular requirements of the organization in question.

A good cover letter should supplement the résumé and motivate the reader to review the résumé. The format shown in Exhibit 2.3 (see page 34) is only a suggestion to help you decide what information to include in a cover letter.

Begin the cover letter with your street address six lines down from the top. Leave three to five lines between the date and the name of the person to whom you are addressing the cover letter. Make sure you leave one blank line between the salutation and the body of the letter and between paragraphs. After typing "Sincerely," leave four blank lines and type your name. This should leave plenty of room for your signature. A sample cover letter is shown in Exhibit 2.4 on pages 35–36.

The following guidelines will help you write good cover letters:

1. Be sure to type your letter neatly; ensure there are no misspellings.
2. Avoid unusual typefaces, such as script.
3. Address the letter to an individual, using the person's name and title. To obtain this information, call the company. If answering a blind newspaper advertisement, address the letter "To Whom It May Concern" or omit the salutation.
4. Be sure your cover letter directly indicates the position you are applying for and tells why you are qualified to fill it.
5. Send the original letter, not a photocopy, with your résumé. Keep a copy for your records.
6. Make your cover letter no more than one page.
7. Include a phone number where you can be reached.
8. Avoid trite language and have someone read the letter over to react to its tone, content, and mechanics.
9. For your own information, record the date you send out each letter and résumé.

Exhibit 2.3
COVER LETTER FORMAT

Your Street Address
Your Town, State, Zip
Phone Number
Fax Number
Date   E-mail

Name
Title
Organization
Address

Dear _____:

First Paragraph. In this paragraph state the reason for the letter, name the specific position or type of work you are applying for, and indicate from which resource (career services office, website, newspaper, contact, employment service) you learned of this opening. The first paragraph can also be used to inquire about future openings.

Second Paragraph. Indicate why you are interested in this position, the company, or its products or services, and what you can do for the employer. If you are a recent graduate, explain how your academic background makes you a qualified candidate. Try not to repeat the same information found in the résumé.

Third Paragraph. Refer the reader to the enclosed résumé for more detailed information.

Fourth Paragraph. In this paragraph say what you will do to follow up on your letter. For example, state that you will call by a certain date to set up an interview or to find out if the company will be recruiting in your area. Finish by indicating your willingness to answer any questions the recipient may have. Be sure you have provided your phone number.

Sincerely,

Type your name
Enclosure

Exhibit 2.4
SAMPLE COVER LETTER

13 Locust Street
San Diego, CA 98021
(619) 555-1111
mcampbell@xxx.com

October 12, 2003

Mr. Ken Kochien
Director of Development
Nature Conservancy Preserves
22 Main Street
Lockport, CA 98772

Dear Mr. Kochien:

In May of 2004 I will graduate from the San Diego campus of University College with a bachelor's degree in political science. I read of your opening for a capital campaign manager in *Community Jobs*, and I am very interested in the possibilities it offers. I am writing to explore the opportunity for employment with the Nature Conservancy Preserves.

The advertisement indicated that you are looking for someone capable of coordinating meetings, producing campaign materials, and writing donor acknowledgments. I believe my résumé outlines a work and education history that you will find interesting and relevant. Beginning with office duties and logistics for a renowned science conference for two summers early in high school, I then gained some advertising and graphics experience with a local newspaper and polished my writing skills working on the college weekly newspaper. Courses in psychology have added to my major course work, and I had some excellent relevant experience working in the campus admissions office. I am productive, focused, and produce high-quality work under time constraints.

As you will see by the enclosed résumé, I have had exposure to considerable technology here at college and am thoroughly familiar with all the software and

continued

database systems you mention in your ad. In addition, I have good spreadsheet experience and excellent word processing skills.

I would like to meet with you to discuss how my education and experience would be consistent with your needs. I will contact your office next week to discuss the possibility of an interview. In the meantime, if you have any questions or require additional information, please contact me at my home, (619) 555-9201.

Sincerely,

Mary Campbell
Enclosure

3

Researching Careers and Networking

Many political science majors choose their degree expecting that it will be the ticket to a job after graduation. But "political science" is a vast field, populated with hundreds of job titles you have never heard of before. You know that a political science major has given you an overview of governmental systems, political philosophy, and related subjects. However, you still may be confused as to exactly what kinds of organizations will hire you. Are congressional staff jobs reserved only for political science majors? Where does a political science major fit into a state or federal government agency, planning agency, or nonprofit organization?

What Do They Call the Job You Want?

One reason for confusion is perhaps a mistaken assumption that a college education provides job training. In most cases it does not. Of course, applied fields such as engineering, management, or education provide specific skills for the workplace as well as an education. Regardless, your overall college education exposes you to numerous fields of study and teaches you quantitative reasoning, critical thinking, writing, and speaking, all of which can be successfully applied to a number of different job fields. But it still remains up to you to choose a job field and you must become skilled at articulating the benefits of your education in a way the prospective employer will appreciate.

Collect Job Titles

The world of employment is a complex place, so you need to become a bit of an explorer and adventurer and be willing to try a variety of techniques to develop a list of possible occupations that might use your talents and education. You might find computerized interest inventories, reference books and other sources, and classified ads helpful in this respect. Once you have a list of possibilities that you are interested in and qualified for, you can move on to find out what kinds of organizations have these job titles.

Computerized Interest Inventories. One way to begin collecting job titles is to identify a number of jobs that call for your degree and the particular skills and interests you identified as part of the self-assessment process. There are excellent interactive career-guidance programs on the market to help you produce such selected lists of possible job titles. Most of these are available at colleges and at some larger town and city libraries. Two of the industry leaders are *CHOICES* and *DISCOVER*. Both allow you to enter interests, values, educational background, and other information to produce lists of possible occupations and industries. Each of the resources listed here will produce different job title lists. Some job titles will appear again and again, while others will be unique to a particular source. Investigate all of them!

Reference Sources. Books on the market that may be available through your local library or career counseling office also suggest various occupations related to specific majors. The following are only a few of the many good books on the market: *The College Board Guide to 150 Popular College Majors, College Majors and Careers: A Resource Guide for Effective Life Planning* both by Paul Phifer, and *Kaplan's What to Study: 101 Fields in a Flash.* All of these books list possible job titles within the academic major.

Political science majors can find a variety of job titles in reference works listing occupational titles. In the *Occupational Outlook Handbook*, for example, a look at major job categories can reveal other jobs. Under the entry for "lawyers," the bulk of the information covers different types of lawyers such as district attorney, patent lawyer, insurance attorney, probate lawyer, tax attorney, title attorney, and more.

At the same time, you can also find some positions you may not have thought about. Their work is related to that of lawyers, but duties differ. Listed under "Related Occupations" you will find paralegal and legal assistant, law clerk, title examiner, arbitrator, mediator and conciliator, and other titles. If you're interested in a legal career, the *Occupational Outlook Handbook* adds some depth to your search by suggesting a number of different occupational directions.

Each job title deserves your consideration. Like removing the layers of an onion, the search for job titles can go on and on! As you spend time doing this activity, you are actually learning more about the value of your degree. What's important in your search at this point is not to become critical or selective but rather to develop as long a list of possibilities as you can. Every source used will help you add new and potentially exciting jobs to your growing list.

Classified Ads. It has been well publicized that the classified ad section of the newspaper represents only a small fraction of the current job market. Nevertheless, the weekly classified ads can be a great help to you in your search. Although they may not be the best place to look for a job, they can teach you a lot about the job market. Classified ads provide a good education in job descriptions, duties, responsibilities, and qualifications. In addition, they provide insight into which industries are actively recruiting and some indication of the area's employment market. This is particularly helpful when seeking a position in a specific geographic area and/or a specific field. For your purposes, classified ads are a good source for job titles to add to your list.

Read the Sunday classified ads in a major market newspaper for several weeks in a row. Cut and paste all the ads that interest you and seem to call for something close to your education, skills, experience, and interests. Remember that classified ads are written for what an organization *hopes* to find, you don't have to meet absolutely every criterion. However, if certain requirements are stated as absolute minimums and you cannot meet them, it's best not to waste your time and that of the employer.

The weekly classified want ads exercise is important because these jobs are out in the marketplace. They truly exist, and people with your qualifications are being sought to apply. What's more, many of these advertisements describe the duties and responsibilities of the job advertised and give you a beginning sense of the challenges and opportunities such a position presents. Some will indicate salary, and that will be helpful as well. This information will better define the jobs for you and provide some good material for possible interviews in that field.

Explore Job Descriptions

Once you've arrived at a solid list of possible job titles that interest you and for which you believe you are somewhat qualified, it's a good idea to do some research on each of these jobs. The preeminent source for such job information is the *Dictionary of Occupational Titles*, or *DOT* (wave.net/upg/immigration/dot_index.html). This directory lists every conceivable job and provides excellent up-to-date information on duties and responsibilities, interactions with associates, and day-to-day assignments and tasks. These descriptions provide a thorough job analysis, but they do not consider the possible employers or the environments in which a job may be performed. So, although a position as public relations officer may be well defined in terms of duties and responsibilities, it does not explain the differences in doing public relations work in a college or a hospital or a factory or a bank. You will need to look somewhere else for work settings.

Learn More About Possible Work Settings

After reading some job descriptions, you may choose to edit and revise your list of job titles once again, discarding those you feel are not suitable and keeping those that continue to hold your interest. Or you may wish to keep your list intact and see where these jobs may be located. For example, if you are interested in public relations and you appear to have those skills and the requisite education, you'll want to know what organizations do public relations. How can you find that out? How much income does someone in public relations make a year and what is the employment potential for the field of public relations?

To answer these and many other questions about your list of job titles, we recommend you try any of the following resources: *Careers Encyclopedia*, the professional societies and resources found throughout this book, *College to Career: The Guide to Job Opportunities*, and the *Occupational Outlook Handbook* (http://stats.bls.gov/ocohome.htm). Each of these resources, in a different way, will help to put the job titles you have selected into an employer context. Perhaps the most extensive discussion is found in the *Occupational Outlook Handbook*, which gives a thorough presentation of the nature of the work, the working conditions, employment statistics, training, other qualifications, and advancement possibilities as well as job outlook and earnings. Related occupations are also detailed, and a select bibliography is provided to help you find additional information.

Continuing with our public relations example, your search through these reference materials would teach you that the public relations jobs you find attractive are available in larger hospitals, financial institutions, most corporations (both consumer goods and industrial goods), media organizations, and colleges and universities.

Networking

Networking is the process of deliberately establishing relationships to get career-related information or to alert potential employers that you are available for work. Networking is critically important to today's job seeker for two reasons: it will help you get the information you need, and it can help you find out about *all* of the available jobs.

Get the Information You Need

Networkers will review your résumé and give you feedback on its effectiveness. They will talk about the job you are looking for and give you a candid appraisal of how they see your strengths and weaknesses. If they have a good sense of the industry or the employment sector for that job, you'll get their feelings on future trends in the industry as well. Some networkers will be very forthcoming about salaries, job-hunting techniques, and suggestions for your job search strategy. Many have been known to place calls right from the interview desk to friends and associates who might be interested in you. Each networker will make his or her own contribution, and each will be valuable.

Because organizations must evolve to adapt to current global market needs, the information provided by decision makers within various organizations will be critical to your success as a new job market entrant. For example, you might learn about the concept of virtual organizations from a networker. Virtual organizations coordinate economic activity to deliver value to customers by using resources outside the traditional boundaries of the organization. This concept is being discussed and implemented by chief executive officers of many organizations, including Ford Motor, Dell, and IBM. Networking can help you find out about this and other trends currently affecting the industries under your consideration.

Find Out About All of the Available Jobs

Not every job that is available at this very moment is advertised for potential applicants to see. This is called the *hidden job market*. Only 15 to 20 percent of all jobs are formally advertised, which means that 80 to 85 percent of available jobs do not appear in published channels. Networking will help you become more knowledgeable about all the employment opportunities available during your job search period.

Although someone you might talk to today doesn't know of any openings within his or her organization, tomorrow or next week or next month an opening may occur. If you've taken the time to show an interest in and knowledge of their organization, if you've shown the company representative how you can help achieve organizational goals and that you can fit into the organization, you'll be one of the first candidates considered for the position.

Networking: A Proactive Approach

Networking is a proactive rather than a reactive approach. You, as a job seeker, are expected to initiate a certain level of activity on your own behalf; you cannot afford to simply respond to jobs listed in the newspaper. Being proactive means building a network of contacts that includes informed and interested decision makers who will provide you with up-to-date knowledge of the current job market and increase your chances of finding out about employment opportunities appropriate for your interests, experience, and level of education. An old axiom of networking says, "You are only two phone calls away from the information you need." In other words, by talking to enough people, you will quickly come across someone who can offer you help.

Preparing to Network

In deliberately establishing relationships, maximize your efforts by organizing your approach. Five specific areas in which you can organize your efforts include reviewing your self-assessment, reviewing your research on job sites and organizations, deciding who it is you want to talk to, keeping track of all your efforts, and creating your self-promotion tools.

Review Your Self-Assessment

Your self-assessment is as important a tool in preparing to network as it has been in other aspects of your job search. You have carefully evaluated your personal traits, personal values, economic needs, longer-term goals, skill base, preferred skills, and underdeveloped skills. During the networking process you will be called upon to communicate what you know about yourself and relate it to the information or job you seek. Be sure to review the exercises that you completed in the self-assessment section of this book in preparation for networking. We've explained that you need to assess what skills you have acquired from your major that are of general value to an employer and to be ready to express those in ways employers can appreciate as useful in their own organizations.

Review Research on Job Sites and Organizations

In addition, individuals assisting you will expect that you'll have at least some background information on the occupation or industry of interest to you. Refer to the appropriate sections of this book and other relevant publications to acquire the background information necessary for effective networking. They'll explain how to identify not only the job titles that might be of interest to you but also what kinds of organizations employ people to do that job. You will develop some sense of working conditions and expectations about duties and responsibilities—all of which will be of help in your networking interviews.

Decide Who It Is You Want to Talk To

Networking cannot begin until you decide who it is that you want to talk to and, in general, what type of information you hope to gain from your contacts. Once you know this, it's time to begin developing a list of contacts. Five useful sources for locating contacts are described here.

College Alumni Network. Most colleges and universities have created a formal network of alumni and friends of the institution who are particularly interested in helping currently enrolled students and graduates of their alma mater gain employment-related information.

It is usually a simple process to make use of an alumni network. Visit your college's website and locate the alumni office and/or your career center. Either or both sites will have information about your school's alumni network. You'll be provided with information on shadowing experiences, geographic information, or those alumni offering job referrals. If you don't find what you're looking for, don't hesitate to phone or E-mail your career center and ask what they can do to help you connect with an alum.

Alumni networkers may provide some combination of the following services: day-long shadowing experiences, telephone interviews, in-person interviews, information on relocating to given geographic areas, internship information, suggestions on graduate school study, and job vacancy notices.

Present and Former Supervisors. If you believe you are on good terms with present or former job supervisors, they may be an excellent resource for providing information or directing you to appropriate resources that would have information related to your current interests and needs. Additionally, these supervisors probably belong to professional organizations that they might be willing to utilize to get information for you.

Employers in Your Area. Although you may be interested in working in a geographic location different from the one where you currently reside, don't overlook the value of the knowledge and contacts those around you are able to provide. Use the local telephone directory and newspaper to identify the types of organizations you are thinking of working for or professionals who have the kinds of jobs you are interested in. Recently, a call made to a local hospital's financial administrator for information on working in health-care financial administration yielded more pertinent information on training seminars, regional professional organizations, and potential employment sites than a national organization was willing to provide.

Employers in Geographic Areas Where You Hope to Work. If you are thinking about relocating, identifying prospective employers or informational contacts in the new location will be critical to your success. Here are some tips for online searching. First, use a "metasearch" engine to get the most out of your search. Metasearch engines combine several engines into one powerful tool. We frequently use dogpile.com and metasearch.com for this purpose. Try using the city and state as your keywords in a search. *New Haven, Connecticut* will bring you to the city's website with links to the chamber of commerce, member businesses, and other valuable resources. By using looksmart.com you can locate newspapers in any area, and they, too, can provide valuable insight before you relocate. Of course, both dogpile and metasearch can lead you to yellow and white page directories in areas you are considering.

Professional Associations and Organizations. Professional associations and organizations can provide valuable information in several areas: career paths that you might not have considered, qualifications relating to those career choices, publications that list current job openings, and workshops or seminars that will enhance your professional knowledge and skills. They can also be excellent sources for background information on given industries: their health, current problems, and future challenges.

There are several excellent resources available to help you locate professional associations and organizations that would have information to meet your needs. Two especially useful publications are the *Encyclopedia of Associations* and *National Trade and Professional Associations of the United States.*

Keep Track of All Your Efforts

It can be difficult, almost impossible, to remember all the details related to each contact you make during the networking process, so you will want to develop a record-keeping system that works for you. Formalize this process by using your computer to keep a record of the people and organizations you want to contact. You can simply record the contact's name, address, and telephone number, and what information you hope to gain.

You could record this as a simple Word document and you could still use the "Find" function if you were trying to locate some data and could only recall the firm's name or the contact's name. If you're comfortable with database management and you have some database software on your computer, then you can put information at your fingertips even if you have only the zip code! The point here is not technological sophistication but good record keeping.

Once you have created this initial list, it will be helpful to keep more detailed information as you begin to actually make the contacts. Those details should include complete contact information, the date and content of each contact, names and information for additional networkers, and required follow-up. Don't forget to send a letter thanking your contact for his or her time! Your contact will appreciate your recall of details of your meetings and conversations, and the information will help you to focus your networking efforts.

Create Your Self-Promotion Tools

There are two types of promotional tools that are used in the networking process. The first is a résumé and cover letter, and the second is a one-minute "infomercial," which may be given over the telephone or in person.

Techniques for writing an effective résumé and cover letter are discussed in Chapter 2. Once you have reviewed that material and prepared these important documents, you will have created one of your self-promotion tools.

The one-minute infomercial will demand that you begin tying your interests, abilities, and skills to the people or organizations you want to network with. Think about your goal for making the contact to help you understand what you should say about yourself. You should be able to express yourself easily and convincingly. If, for example, you are contacting an alumnus of your institution to obtain the names of possible employment sites in a distant city, be prepared to discuss why you are interested in moving to that location, the types of jobs you are interested in, and the skills and abilities you possess that will make you a qualified candidate.

To create a meaningful one-minute infomercial, write it out, practice it as if it will be a spoken presentation, rewrite it, and practice it again if necessary until expressing yourself comes easily and is convincing.

Here's a simplified example of an infomercial for use over the telephone:

Hello, Mr. Hamrick? My name is Cindy Lewis. I am a recent graduate of Gulf Shores College, and I wish to enter the nonprofit field. I feel confident I have many of the skills valued by managers in nonprofit settings. These include strong quantitative skills with solid research and computer experience. In addition, I have excellent interpersonal skills and am known as a compassionate, caring individual. I understand these are valuable traits in your line of work.

Mr. Hamrick, I'm calling you because I still need more information about nonprofit management and where I might fit in. I'm hoping you'll have time to sit down with me for about half an hour and discuss your perspective on careers in nonprofit management with me. There are so many possible employers to approach, and I am seeking some advice on which might be the best bet for my particular combination of skills and experience.

Would you be willing to talk with me? I would greatly appreciate it. I am available most mornings, if that's convenient for you.

It very well may happen that your employer contact wishes you to communicate by E-mail. The infomercial quoted above could easily be rewritten for an E-mail message. You should "cut and paste" your résumé right into the E-mail text itself.

Other effective self-promotion tools include portfolios for those in the arts, writing professions, or teaching. Portfolios show examples of work, photographs of projects or classroom activities, or certificates and credentials that are job related. There may not be an opportunity to use the portfolio during an interview, and it is not something that should be left with the organization. It is designed to be explained and displayed by the creator. However, during some networking meetings, there may be an opportunity to illustrate a point or strengthen a qualification by exhibiting the portfolio.

Beginning the Networking Process

Set the Tone for Your Communications
It can be useful to establish "tone words" for any communications you embark upon. Before making your first telephone call or writing your first letter, decide what you want the person to think of you. If you are networking to try to obtain a job, your tone words might include descriptors such as *genuine*, *informed*, and *self-knowledgeable*. When you're trying to acquire information, your tone words may have a slightly different focus, such as *courteous*, *organized*, *focused*, and *well-spoken*. Use the tone words you establish for your contacts to guide you through the networking process.

Honestly Express Your Intentions
When contacting individuals, it is important to be honest about your reasons for making the contact. Establish your purpose in your own mind and be able and ready to articulate it concisely. Determine an initial agenda, whether it be informational questioning or self-promotion, present it to your contact, and be ready to respond immediately. If you don't adequately prepare before initiating your overture, you may find yourself at a disadvantage if you're asked to immediately begin your informational interview or self-promotion during the first phone conversation or visit.

Start Networking Within Your Circle of Confidence
Once you have organized your approach—by utilizing specific researching methods, creating a system for keeping track of the people you will contact, and developing effective self-promotion tools—you are ready to begin networking. The best way to begin networking is by talking with a group of people you trust and feel comfortable with. This group is usually made up of your family, friends, and career counselors. No matter who is in this inner circle, they will have a special interest in seeing you succeed in your job search. In addition, because they will be easy to talk to, you should try taking some risks in terms of practicing your information-seeking approach. Gain confidence in talking about the strengths you bring to an organization and the underdeveloped skills you feel hinder your candidacy. Be sure to review the section on self-assessment for tips on approaching each of these areas.

Ask for critical but constructive feedback from the people in your circle of confidence on the letters you write and the one-minute infomercial you have developed. Evaluate whether you want to make the changes they suggest, then practice the changes on others within this circle.

Stretch the Boundaries of Your Networking Circle of Confidence

Once you have refined the promotional tools you will use to accomplish your networking goals, you will want to make additional contacts. Because you will not know most of these people, it will be a less comfortable activity to undertake. The practice that you gained with your inner circle of trusted friends should have prepared you to now move outside of that comfort zone.

It is said that any information a person needs is only two phone calls away, but the information cannot be gained until you (1) make a reasonable guess about who might have the information you need and (2) pick up the telephone to make the call. Using your network list that includes alumni, instructors, supervisors, employers, and associations, you can begin preparing your list of questions that will allow you to get the information you need.

Prepare the Questions You Want to Ask

Networkers can provide you with the insider's perspective on any given field and you can ask them questions that you might not want to ask in an interview. For example, you can ask them to describe the more repetitious or mundane parts of the job or ask them for a realistic idea of salary expectations. Be sure to prepare your questions ahead of time so that you are organized and efficient.

Be Prepared to Answer Some Questions

To communicate effectively, you must anticipate questions that will be asked of you by the networkers you contact. Revisit the self-assessment process you undertook and the research you've done so that you can effortlessly respond to questions about your short- and long-term goals and the kinds of jobs you are most interested in pursuing.

General Networking Tips

Make Every Contact Count. Setting the tone for each interaction is critical. Approaches that will help you communicate in an effective way include politeness, being appreciative of time provided to you, and being prepared and thorough. Remember, *everyone* within an organization has a circle of influence, so be prepared to interact effectively with each person you encounter in the networking process, including secretarial and support staff. Many information or job seekers have thwarted their own efforts by being rude to some individuals they encountered as they networked because they made the incorrect assumption that certain persons were unimportant.

Sometimes your contacts may be surprised at their ability to help you. After meeting and talking with you, they might think they have not offered much in the way of help. A day or two later, however, they may make a contact that would be useful to you and refer you to that person.

With Each Contact, Widen Your Circle of Networkers. Always leave an informational interview with the names of at least two more people who can help you get the information or job that you are seeking. Don't be shy about asking for additional contacts; networking is all about increasing the number of people you can interact with to achieve your goals.

Make Your Own Decisions. As you talk with different people and get answers to the questions you pose, you may hear conflicting information or get conflicting suggestions. Your job is to listen to these "experts" and decide what information and which suggestions will help you achieve *your* goals. Only implement those suggestions that you believe will work for you.

Shutting Down Your Network

As you achieve the goals that motivated your networking activity—getting the information you need or the job you want—the time will come to inactivate all or parts of your network. As you do, be sure to tell your primary supporters about your change in status. Call or write to each one of them and give them as many details about your new status as you feel is necessary to maintain a positive relationship.

Because a network takes on a life of its own, activity undertaken on your behalf will continue even after you cease your efforts. As you get calls or are contacted in some fashion, be sure to inform these networkers about your change in status, and thank them for assistance they have provided.

Information on the latest employment trends indicates that workers will change jobs or careers several times in their lifetime. Networking, then, will be a critical aspect in the span of your professional life. If you carefully and thoughtfully conduct your networking activities during your job search, you will have a solid foundation of experience when you need to network the next time around.

Where Are These Jobs, Anyway?

Having a list of job titles that you've designed around your own career interests and skills is an excellent beginning. It means you've really thought about who you are and what you are presenting to the employment market. It has caused you to think seriously about the most appealing environments to work in, and you have identified some employer types that represent these environments.

The research and the thinking that you've done thus far will be used again and again. They will be helpful in writing your résumé and cover letters, in talking about yourself on the telephone to prospective employers, and in answering interview questions.

Now is a good time to begin to narrow the field of job titles and employment sites down to some specific employers to initiate the employment contact.

Find Out Which Employers Hire People Like You

This section will provide tips, techniques, and specific resources for developing an actual list of specific employers that can be used to make contacts. It is only an outline that you must be prepared to tailor to your own particular needs and according to what you bring to the job search. Once again, it is important to communicate with others along the way exactly what you're looking for and what your goals are for the research you're doing. Librarians, employers, career counselors, friends, friends of friends, business contacts, and bookstore staff will all have helpful information on geographically specific and new resources to aid you in locating employers who'll hire you.

Identify Information Resources

Your interview wardrobe and your new résumé might have put a dent in your wallet, but the resources you'll need to pursue your job search are available for free. The categories of information detailed here are not hard to find and are yours for the browsing.

Numerous resources described in this section will help you identify actual employers. Use all of them or any others that you identify as available in your geographic area. As you become experienced in this process, you'll quickly figure out which information sources are helpful and which are not. If you live in a rural area, a well-planned day trip to a major city that includes a college career office, a large college or city library, state and federal employment centers, a chamber of commerce office, and a well-stocked bookstore can produce valuable results.

There are many excellent resources available to help you identify actual job sites. They are categorized into employer directories (usually indexed by product lines and geographic location), geographically based directories (designed to highlight particular cities, regions, or states), career-specific directories (e.g., *Sports MarketPlace*, which lists tens of thousands of firms involved with sports), periodicals and newspapers, targeted job posting publications, and videos. This is by no means meant to be a complete treatment of resources but rather a starting point for identifying useful resources.

Working from the more general references to highly specific resources, we provide a basic list to help you begin your search. Many of these you'll find easily available. In some cases reference librarians and others will suggest even better materials for your particular situation. Start to create your own customized bibliography of job search references.

Geographically Based Directories. The Job Bank series published by Bob Adams, Inc. (aip.com) contains detailed entries on each area's major employers, including business activity, address, phone number, and hiring contact name. Many listings specify educational backgrounds being sought in potential employees. Each volume contains a solid discussion of each city's or state's major employment sectors. Organizations are also indexed by industry. Job Bank volumes are available for the following places: Atlanta, Boston, Chicago, Dallas–Ft. Worth, Denver, Detroit, Florida, Houston, Los Angeles, Minneapolis, New York, Ohio, Philadelphia, San Francisco, Seattle, St. Louis, Washington, D.C., and other cities throughout the Northwest.

National Job Bank (careercity.com) lists employers in every state, along with contact names and commonly hired job categories. Included are many small companies often overlooked by other directories. Companies are also indexed by industry. This publication provides information on educational backgrounds sought and lists company benefits.

Periodicals and Newspapers. Several sources are available to help you locate which journals or magazines carry job advertisements in your field. Other resources help you identify opportunities in other parts of the country.

- *Where the Jobs Are: A Comprehensive Directory of 1200 Journals Listing Career Opportunities*
- *Corptech Fast 5000 Company Locator*
- *National Ad Search* (nationaladsearch.com)
- *The Federal Jobs Digest* (jobsfed.com) and *Federal Career Opportunities*
- *World Chamber of Commerce Directory* (chamberofcommerce.org)

This list is certainly not exhaustive; use it to begin your job search work.

Targeted Job Posting Publications. Although the resources that follow are national in scope, they are either targeted to one medium of contact (telephone), focused on specific types of jobs, or less comprehensive than the sources previously listed.

- *Job Hotlines USA* (careers.org/topic/01_002.html)
- *The Job Hunter* (jobhunter.com)
- *Current Jobs for Graduates* (graduatejobs.com)
- *Environmental Opportunities* (ecojobs.com)
- *Y National Vacancy List* (ymcahrm.ns.ca/employed/ jobleads.html)
- *ARTSearch*
- *Community Jobs*
- *National Association of Colleges and Employers: Job Choices series*
- *National Association of Colleges and Employers* (naceweb.org)

Videos. You may be one of the many job seekers who likes to get information via a medium other than paper. Many career libraries, public libraries, and career centers in libraries carry an assortment of videos that will help you learn new techniques and get information helpful in the job search.

Locate Information Resources
Throughout these introductory chapters, we have continually referred you to various websites for information on everything from job listings to career information. Using the Web gives you a mobility at your computer that you don't enjoy if you rely solely on books or newspapers or printed journals.

Moreover, material on the Web, if the site is maintained, can be the most up-to-date information available.

You'll eventually identify the information resources that work best for you, but make certain you've covered the full range of resources before you begin to rely on a smaller list. Here's a short list of informational sites that many job seekers find helpful:

- Public and college libraries
- College career centers
- Bookstores
- The Internet
- Local and state government personnel offices
- Career/job fairs

Each one of these sites offers a collection of resources that will help you get the information you need.

As you meet and talk with service professionals at all these sites, be sure to let them know what you're doing. Inform them of your job search, what you've already accomplished, and what you're looking for. The more people who know you're job seeking, the greater the possibility that someone will have information or know someone who can help you along your way.

4

Interviewing and Job Offer Considerations

Certainly, there can be no one part of the job search process more fraught with anxiety and worry than the interview. Yet seasoned job seekers welcome the interview and will often say, "Just get me an interview and I'm on my way!" They understand that the interview is crucial to the hiring process and equally crucial for them, as job candidates, to have the opportunity of a personal dialogue to add to what the employer may already have learned from the résumé, cover letter, and telephone conversations.

Believe it or not, the interview is to be welcomed, and even enjoyed! It is a perfect opportunity for you, the candidate, to sit down with an employer and express yourself and display who you are and what you want. Of course, it takes thought and planning and a little strategy; after all, it *is* a job interview! But it can be a positive, if not pleasant, experience and one you can look back on and feel confident about your performance and effort.

For many new job seekers, a job, any job, seems a wonderful thing. But seasoned interview veterans know that the job interview is an important step for both sides—the employer and the candidate—to see what each has to offer and whether there is going to be a "fit" of personalities, work styles, and attitudes. And it is this concept of balance in the interview, that both sides have important parts to play, that holds the key to success in mastering this aspect of the job search strategy.

Try to think of the interview as a conversation between two interested and equal partners. You both have important, even vital, information to deliver and to learn. Of course, there's no denying the employer has some leverage, especially in the initial interview for recruitment or any interview scheduled by the candidate and not the recruiter. That should not prevent the interviewee from seeking to play an equal part in what should be a fair exchange of information. Too often the untutored candidate allows the interview to become one-sided. The employer asks all the questions and the candidate simply responds. The ideal would be for two mutually interested parties to sit down and discuss possibilities for each. This is a conversation of significance, and it requires preparation, thought about the tone of the interview, and planning of the nature and details of the information to be exchanged.

Preparing for the Interview

The length of most initial interviews is about thirty minutes. Given the brevity, the information that is exchanged ought to be important. The candidate should be delivering material that the employer cannot discover on the résumé, and in turn, the candidate should be learning things about the employer that he or she could not otherwise find out. After all, if you have only thirty minutes, why waste time on information that is already published? The information exchanged is more than just factual, and both sides will learn much from what they see of each other, as well. How the candidate looks, speaks, and acts are important to the employer. The employer's attention to the interview and awareness of the candidate's résumé, the setting, and the quality of information presented are important to the candidate.

Just as the employer has every right to be disappointed when a prospect is late for the interview, looks unkempt, and seems ill-prepared to answer fairly standard questions, the candidate may be disappointed with an interviewer who isn't ready for the meeting, hasn't learned the basic résumé facts, and is constantly interrupted by telephone calls. In either situation there's good reason to feel let down.

There are many elements to a successful interview, and some of them are not easy to describe or prepare for. Sometimes there is just a chemistry between interviewer and interviewee that brings out the best in both, and a good exchange takes place. But there is much the candidate can do to pave the way for success in terms of his or her résumé, personal appearance, goals, and interview strategy—each of which we will discuss. However, none of this preparation is as important as the time and thought the candidate gives to personal self-assessment.

Self-Assessment

Neither a stunning résumé nor an expensive, well-tailored suit can compensate for candidates who do not know what they want, where they are going, or why they are interviewing with a particular employer. Self-assessment, the process by which we begin to know and acknowledge our own particular blend of education, experiences, needs, and goals, is not something that can be sorted out the weekend before a major interview. Of all the elements of interview preparation, this one requires the longest lead time and cannot be faked.

Because the time allotted for most interviews is brief, it is all the more important for job candidates to understand and express succinctly why they are there and what they have to offer. This is not a time for undue modesty (or for braggadocio either); it is a time for a compelling, reasoned statement of why you feel that you and this employer might make a good match. It means you have to have thought about your skills, interests, and attributes; related those to your life experiences and your own history of challenges and opportunities; and determined what that indicates about your strengths, preferences, values, and areas needing further development.

If you need some assistance with self-assessment issues, refer to Chapter 1. Included are suggested exercises that can be done as needed, such as making up an experiential diary and extracting obvious strengths and weaknesses from past experiences. These simple assignments will help you look at past activities as collections of tasks with accompanying skills and responsibilities. Don't overlook your high school or college career office. Many offer personal counseling on self-assessment issues and may provide testing instruments such as the *Myers-Briggs Type Indicator (MBTI)*, the *Harrington-O'Shea Career Decision-Making System (CDM)*, the *Strong Interest Inventory (SII)*, or any other of a wide selection of assessment tools that can help you clarify some of these issues prior to the interview stage of your job search.

The Résumé
Résumé preparation has been discussed in detail, and some basic examples were provided. In this section we want to concentrate on how best to use your résumé in the interview. In most cases the employer will have seen the résumé prior to the interview, and, in fact, it may well have been the quality of that résumé that secured the interview opportunity.

An interview is a conversation, however, and not an exercise in reading. So, if the employer hasn't seen your résumé and you have brought it along to the interview, wait until asked or until the end of the interview to offer it. Otherwise, you may find yourself staring at the back of your résumé and simply answering "yes" and "no" to a series of questions drawn from that document.

Sometimes an interviewer is not prepared and does not know or recall the contents of the résumé and may use the résumé to a greater or lesser degree as a "prompt" during the interview. It is for you to judge what that may indicate about the individual performing the interview or the employer. If your interviewer seems surprised by the scheduled meeting, relies on the résumé to an inordinate degree, and seems otherwise unfamiliar with your background, this lack of preparation for the hiring process could well be a symptom of general management disorganization or may simply be the result of poor planning on the part of one individual. It is your responsibility as a potential employee to be aware of these signals and make your decisions accordingly.

In any event, it is perfectly acceptable for you to get the conversation back to a more interpersonal style by saying something like, "Mr. Smith, you might be interested in some recent experience I gained in an internship that is not detailed on my résumé. May I tell you about it?" This can return the interview to two people talking to each other, not one reading and the other responding.

By all means, bring at least one copy of your résumé to the interview. Occasionally, at the close of an interview, an interviewer will express an interest in circulating a résumé to several departments, and you could then offer the copy you brought. Sometimes, an interview appointment provides an opportunity to meet others in the organization who may express an interest in you and your background, and it may be helpful to follow up with a copy of your résumé. Our best advice, however, is to keep it out of sight until needed or requested.

Employer Information

Whether your interview is for graduate school admission, an overseas corporate position, or a position with a local company, it is important to know something about the employer or the organization. Keeping in mind that the interview is relatively brief and that you will hopefully have other interviews with other organizations, it is important to keep your research in proportion. If secondary interviews are called for, you will have additional time to do further research. For the first interview, it is helpful to know the organization's mission, goals, size, scope of operations, and so forth. Your research may uncover recent areas of challenge or particular successes that may help to fuel the interview. Use the "What Do They Call the Job You Want?" section of Chapter 3, your library, and your career or guidance office to help you locate this information in the most efficient way possible. Don't be shy in asking advice of these counseling and guidance professionals on how best to spend your preparation time. With some practice, you'll soon learn how much information is enough and which kinds of information are most useful to you.

Interview Content

We've already discussed how it can help to think of the interview as an important conversation—one that, as with any conversation, you want to find pleasant and interesting and to leave you with a good feeling. But because this conversation is especially important, the information that's exchanged is critical to its success. What do you want them to know about you? What do you need to know about them? What interview technique do you need to particularly pay attention to? How do you want to manage the close of the interview? What steps will follow in the hiring process?

Except for the professional interviewer, most of us find interviewing stressful and anxiety-provoking. Developing a strategy before you begin interviewing will help you relieve some stress and anxiety. One particular strategy that has worked for many and may work for you is interviewing by objective. Before you interview, write down three to five goals you would like to achieve for that interview. They may be technique goals: smile a little more, have a firmer handshake, be sure to ask about the next stage in the interview process before leaving. They may be content-oriented goals: find out about the company's current challenges and opportunities; be sure to speak of your recent research, writing experiences, or foreign travel. Whatever your goals, jot down a few of them as goals for each interview.

Most people find that in trying to achieve these few goals, their interviewing technique becomes more organized and focused. After the interview, the most common question friends and family ask is "How did it go?" With this technique, you have an indication of whether you met *your* goals for the meeting, not just some vague idea of how it went. Chances are, if you accomplished what you wanted to, it improved the quality of the entire interview. As you continue to interview, you will want to revise your goals to continue improving your interview skills.

Now, add to the concept of the significant conversation the idea of a beginning, a middle, and a closing and you will have two thoughts that will give your interview a distinctive character. Be sure to make your introduction warm and cordial. Say your full name (and if it's a difficult-to-pronounce name, help the interviewer to pronounce it) and make certain you know your interviewer's name and how to pronounce it. Most interviews begin with some "soft talk" about the weather, chat about the candidate's trip to the interview site, or national events. This is done as a courtesy to relax both you and the interviewer, to get you talking, and to generally try to defuse the atmosphere of excessive tension. Try to be yourself, engage in the conversation, and don't try to second-guess the interviewer. This is simply what it appears to be—casual conversation.

Once you and the interviewer move on to exchange more serious information in the middle part of the interview, the two most important concerns become your ability to handle challenging questions and your success at asking meaningful ones. Interviewer questions will probably fall into one of three categories: personal assessment and career direction, academic assessment, and knowledge of the employer. Here are a few examples of questions in each category:

Personal Assessment and Career Direction
1. What motivates you to put forth your best effort?
2. What do you consider to be your greatest strengths and weaknesses?
3. What qualifications do you have that make you think you will be successful in this career?

Academic Assessment
1. What led you to choose your major?
2. What subjects did you like best and least? Why?
3. How has your college experience prepared you for this career?

Knowledge of the Employer
1. What do you think it takes to be successful in an organization like ours?
2. In what ways do you think you can make a contribution to our organization?
3. Why did you choose to seek a position with this organization?

The interviewer wants a response to each question but is also gauging your enthusiasm, preparedness, and willingness to communicate. In each response you should provide some information about yourself that can be related to the employer's needs. A common mistake is to give too much information. Answer each question completely, but be careful not to run on too long with extensive details or examples.

Questions About Underdeveloped Skills

Most employers interview people who have met some minimum criteria of education and experience. They interview candidates to see who they are, to learn what kind of personality they exhibit, and to get some sense of how this person might fit into the existing organization. It may be that you are asked about skills the employer hopes to find and that you have not documented. Maybe it's grant-writing experience, knowledge of the European political system, or a knowledge of the film world.

To questions about skills and experiences you don't have, answer honestly and forthrightly and try to offer some additional information about skills you do have. For example, perhaps the employer is disappointed you have no grant-writing experience. An honest answer may be as follows:

No, unfortunately, I was never in a position to acquire those skills. I do understand something of the complexities of the grant-writing process and feel confident that my attention to detail, careful reading skills, and strong writing would make grants a wonderful challenge in a new job. I think I could get up on the learning curve quickly.

The employer hears an honest admission of lack of experience but is reassured by some specific skill details that do relate to grant writing and a confident manner that suggests enthusiasm and interest in a challenge.

For many students, questions about their possible contribution to an employer's organization can prove challenging. Because your education has probably not included specific training for a job, you need to review your academic record and select capabilities you have developed in your major that an employer can appreciate. For example, perhaps you read well and can analyze and condense what you've read into smaller, more focused pieces. That could be valuable. Or maybe you did some serious research and you know you have valuable investigative skills. Your public speaking might be highly developed and you might use visual aids appropriately and effectively. Or maybe your skill at correspondence, memos, and messages is effective. Whatever it is, you must take it out of the academic context and put it into a new, employer-friendly context so your interviewer can best judge how you could help the organization.

Exhibiting knowledge of the organization will, without a doubt, show the interviewer that you are interested enough in the available position to have done some legwork in preparation for the interview. Remember, it is not necessary to know every detail of the organization's history but rather to have a general knowledge about why it is in business and how the industry is faring.

Sometime during the interview, generally after the midway point, you'll be asked if you have any questions for the interviewer. Your questions will tell the employer much about your attitude and your desire to understand the organization's expectations so you can compare them to your own strengths. The following are just a few questions you might want to ask:

1. What is the communication style of the organization? (meetings, memos, and so forth)
2. What would a typical day in this position be like for me?
3. What have been some of the interesting challenges and opportunities your organization has recently faced?

Most interviews draw to a natural closing point, so be careful not to prolong the discussion. At a signal from the interviewer, wind up your presentation, express your appreciation for the opportunity, and be sure to ask what the next stage in the process will be. When can you expect to hear from them? Will they be conducting second-tier interviews? If you are interested and haven't heard, would they mind a phone call? Be sure to collect a business card with the name and phone number of your interviewer. On your way out, you might have an opportunity to pick up organizational literature you haven't seen before.

With the right preparation—a thorough self-assessment, professional clothing, and employer information—you'll be able to set and achieve the goals you have established for the interview process.

Interview Follow-Up

Quite often there is a considerable time lag between interviewing for a position and being hired or, in the case of the networker, between your phone call or letter to a possible contact and the opportunity of a meeting. This can be frustrating. "Why aren't they contacting me?" "I thought I'd get another interview, but no one has telephoned." "Am I out of the running?" You don't know what is happening.

Consider the Differing Perspectives

Of course, there is another perspective—that of the networker or hiring organization. Organizations are complex, with multiple tasks that need to be accomplished each day. Hiring is a discrete activity that does not occur as frequently as other job assignments. The hiring process might have to take second place to other, more immediate organizational needs. Although it may be very important to you, and it is certainly ultimately significant to the employer, other issues such as fiscal management, planning and product development, employer vacation periods, or financial constraints may prevent an organization or individual within that organization from acting on your employment or your request for information as quickly as you or they would prefer.

Use Your Communication Skills

Good communication is essential here to resolve any anxieties, and the responsibility is on you, the job or information seeker. Too many job seekers and networkers offer as an excuse that they don't want to "bother" the organization by writing letters or calling. Let us assure you here and now, once and for all, that if you are troubling an organization by over-communicating, someone will indicate that situation to you quite clearly. If not, you can only assume you are a worthwhile prospect and the employer appreciates being reminded of your availability and interest. Let's look at follow-up practices in the job interview process and the networking situation separately.

Following Up on the Employment Interview

A brief thank-you note following an interview is an excellent and polite way to begin a series of follow-up communications with a potential employer with whom you have interviewed and want to remain in touch. It should be just that—a thank-you for a good meeting. If you failed to mention some fact or experience during your interview that you think might add to your candidacy, you may use this note to do that. However, this should be essentially a note whose overall tone is appreciative and, if appropriate, indicative of a continuing interest in pursuing any opportunity that may exist with that organization. It is one of the few pieces of business correspondence that may be handwritten, but always use plain, good-quality, standard-size paper.

If, however, at this point you are no longer interested in the employer, the thank-you note is an appropriate time to indicate that. You are under no obligation to identify any reason for not continuing to pursue employment with that organization, but if you are so inclined to indicate your professional reasons (pursuing other employers more akin to your interests, looking for greater income production than this employer can provide, a different geographic location), you certainly may. It should not be written with an eye to negotiation, for it will not be interpreted as such.

As part of your interview closing, you should have taken the initiative to establish lines of communication for continuing information about your candidacy. If you asked permission to telephone, wait a week following your thank-you note, then telephone your contact simply to inquire how things are progressing on your employment status. The feedback you receive here should be taken at face value. If your interviewer simply has no information, he or she will tell you so and indicate whether you should call again and when. Don't be discouraged if this should continue over some period of time.

If during this time something occurs that you think improves or changes your candidacy (some new qualification or experience you may have had), including any offers from other organizations, by all means telephone or write to inform the employer about this. In the case of an offer from a competing but less desirable or equally desirable organization, telephone your contact, explain what has happened, express your real interest in the organization, and inquire whether some determination on your employment might be made before you must respond to this other offer. An organization that is truly interested in you may be moved to make a decision about your candidacy. Equally possible is the scenario in which they are not yet ready to make a decision and so advise you to take the offer that has been presented. Again, you have no ethical alternative but to deal with the information presented in a straightforward manner.

When accepting other employment, be sure to contact any employers still actively considering you and inform them of your new job. Thank them graciously for their consideration. There are many other job seekers out there just like you who will benefit from having their candidacy improved when others bow out of the race. Who knows, you might at some future time have occasion to interact professionally with one of the organizations with which you sought employment. How embarrassing it would be to have someone remember you as the candidate who failed to notify them that you were taking a job elsewhere!

In all of your follow-up communications, keep good notes of whom you spoke with, when you called, and any instructions that were given about return communications. This will prevent any misunderstandings and provide you with good records of what has transpired.

Job Offer Considerations

For many recent college graduates, the thrill of their first job and, for some, the most substantial regular income they have ever earned seems an excess of good fortune coming at once. To question that first income or to be critical in any way of the conditions of employment at the time of the initial offer seems like looking a gift horse in the mouth. It doesn't seem to occur to many new hires even to attempt to negotiate any aspect of their first job. And, as many employers who deal with entry-level jobs for recent college graduates will readily confirm, the reality is that there simply isn't much movement in salary available to these new college recruits. The entry-level hire generally does not have an employment track record on a professional level to provide any leverage for negotiation. Real negotiations on salary, benefits, retirement provisions, and so forth come to those with significant employment records at higher income levels.

Of course, the job offer is more than just money. It can be composed of geographic assignment, duties and responsibilities, training, benefits, health and medical insurance, educational assistance, car allowance or company vehicle, and a host of other items. All of this is generally detailed in the formal letter that presents the final job offer. In most cases this is a follow-up to a personal phone call from the employer representative who has been principally responsible for your hiring process.

That initial telephone offer is certainly binding as a verbal agreement, but most firms follow up with a detailed letter outlining the most significant parts of your employment contract. You may, of course, choose to respond immediately at the time of the telephone offer (which would be considered a binding oral contract), but you will also be required to formally answer the letter of offer with a letter of acceptance, restating the salient elements of the employer's description of your position, salary, and benefits. This ensures that both parties are clear on the terms and conditions of employment and remuneration and any other outstanding aspects of the job offer.

Is This the Job You Want?

Most new employees will respond affirmatively in writing, glad to be in the position to accept employment. If you've worked hard to get the offer and the job market is tight, other offers may not be in sight, so you will say, "Yes, I accept!" What is important here is that the job offer you accept be one that does fit your particular needs, values, and interests as you've outlined them in your self-assessment process. Moreover, it should be a job that will not only use your skills and education but also challenge you to develop new skills and talents.

Jobs are sometimes accepted too hastily, for the wrong reasons, and without proper scrutiny by the applicant. For example, an individual might readily accept a sales job only to find the continual rejection by potential clients unendurable. An office worker might realize within weeks the constraints of a desk job and yearn for more activity. Employment is an important part of our lives. It is, for most of our adult lives, our most continuous productive activity. We want to make good choices based on the right criteria.

If you have a low tolerance for risk, a job based on commission will certainly be very anxiety-provoking. If being near your family is important, issues of relocation could present a decision crisis for you. If you're an adventurous person, a job with frequent travel would provide needed excitement and be very desirable. The importance of income, the need to continue your education, your personal health situation—all of these have an impact on whether the job you are considering will ultimately meet your needs. Unless you've spent some time understanding and thinking about these issues, it will be difficult to evaluate offers you do receive.

More important, if you make a decision that you cannot tolerate and feel you must leave that job, you will then have both unemployment and self-esteem issues to contend with. These will combine to make the next job search tough going, indeed. So make your acceptance a carefully considered decision.

Negotiate Your Offer

It may be that there is some aspect of your job offer that is not particularly attractive to you. Perhaps there is no relocation allotment to help you move your possessions, and this presents some financial hardship for you. It may be that the health insurance is less than you had hoped. Your initial assignment may be different from what you expected, either in its location or in the duties and responsibilities that comprise it. Or it may simply be that the salary is less than you anticipated. Other considerations may be your official starting date of employment, vacation time, evening hours, dates of training programs or schools, and other concerns.

If you are considering not accepting the job because of some item or items in the job offer "package" that do not meet your needs, you should know that most employers emphatically wish that you would bring that issue to their attention. It may be that the employer can alter it to make the offer more agreeable for you. In some cases it cannot be changed. In any event the employer would generally like to have the opportunity to try to remedy a difficulty rather than risk losing a good potential employee over an issue that might have been resolved. After all, they have spent time and funds in securing your services, and they certainly deserve an opportunity to resolve any possible differences.

Honesty is the best approach in discussing any objections or uneasiness you might have over the employer's offer. Having received your formal offer in writing, contact your employer representative and indicate your particular dissatisfaction in a straightforward manner. For example, you might explain that while you are very interested in being employed by this organization, the salary (or any other benefit) is less than you have determined you require. State the terms you need, and listen to the response. You may be asked to put this in writing, or you may be asked to hold off until the firm can decide on a response. If you are dealing with a senior representative of the organization, one who has been involved in hiring for some time, you may get an immediate response or a solid indication of possible outcomes.

Perhaps the issue is one of relocation. Your initial assignment is in the Midwest, and because you had indicated a strong West Coast preference, you are surprised at the actual assignment. You might simply indicate that while you understand the need for the company to assign you based on its needs, you are disappointed and had hoped to be placed on the West Coast. You could inquire if that were still possible and, if not, would it be reasonable to expect a West Coast relocation in the future.

If your request is presented in a reasonable way, most employers will not see this as jeopardizing your offer. If they can agree to your proposal, they will. If not, they will simply tell you so, and you may choose to continue your candidacy with them or remove yourself from consideration. The choice will be up to you.

Some firms will adjust benefits within their parameters to meet the candidate's need if at all possible. If a candidate requires a relocation cost allowance, he or she may be asked to forgo tuition benefits for the first year to accomplish this adjustment. An increase in life insurance may be adjusted by some other benefit trade-off; perhaps a family dental plan is not needed. In these decisions you are called upon, sometimes under time pressure, to know how you value these issues and how important each is to you.

Many employers find they are more comfortable negotiating for candidates who have unique qualifications or who bring especially needed expertise to the organization. Employers hiring large numbers of entry-level college graduates may be far more reluctant to accommodate any changes in offer conditions. They are well supplied with candidates with similar education and experience so that if rejected by one candidate, they can draw new candidates from an ample labor pool.

Compare Offers

The condition of the economy, the job seeker's academic major and particular geographic job market, and individual needs and demands for certain employment conditions may not provide more than one job offer at a time. Some job seekers may feel that no reasonable offer should go unaccepted for the simple fear there won't be another.

In a tough job market, or if the job you seek is not widely available, or when your job search goes on too long and becomes difficult to sustain financially and emotionally, it may be necessary to accept an inferior offer. The alternative is continued unemployment. Even here, when you feel you don't have a choice, you can at least understand that in accepting this particular offer, there may be limitations and conditions you don't appreciate. At the time of acceptance, there were no other alternatives, but you can begin to use that position to gain the experience and talent to move toward a more attractive position.

Sometimes, however, more than one offer is received, and the candidate has the luxury of choice. If the job seeker knows what he or she wants and has done the necessary self-assessment honestly and thoroughly, it may be clear that one of the offers conforms more closely to those expressed wants and needs.

However, if, as so often happens, the offers are similar in terms of conditions and salary, the question then becomes which organization might provide the necessary climate, opportunities, and advantages for your professional development and growth. This is the time when solid employer research and astute questioning during the interviews really pays off. How much did you learn about the employer through your own research and skillful questioning? When the interviewer asked during the interview "Do you have any questions?" did you ask the kinds of questions that would help resolve a choice between one organization and another? Just as an employer must decide among numerous applicants, so must the applicant learn to assess the potential employer. Both are partners in the job search.

Reneging on an Offer

An especially disturbing occurrence for employers and career counseling professionals is when a job seeker formally (either orally or by written contract) accepts employment with one organization and later reneges on the agreement and goes with another employer.

There are all kinds of rationalizations offered for this unethical behavior. None of them satisfies. The sad irony is that what the job seeker is willing to do to the employer—make a promise and then break it—he or she would be outraged to have done to him- or herself: have the job offer pulled. It is a very bad way to begin a career. It suggests the individual has not taken the time to do the necessary self-assessment and self-awareness exercises to think and judge critically. The new offer taken may, in fact, be no better or worse than the one refused. You should be aware that there have been incidents of legal action following job candidates' reneging on an offer. This adds a very sour note to what should be a harmonious beginning of a lifelong adventure.

PART TWO

THE CAREER PATHS

5

Introduction to the Political Science Career Paths

Government is important to everyone. As a result, the study of government and political institutions, which forms the basis for political science, holds genuine importance not only to academicians, but also to ordinary citizens.

The development and refinement of government has been a long, complex story. Fifty thousand years ago, human beings were largely uncivilized. They hunted animals and gathered fruits and other plant foods, living together in packs or clans. There was no written language and, of course, no formal government.

A witty commentator looking at today's political scene might laugh and say, "Those were the good old days!" But the truth is, life without government was not idyllic. There were no laws to protect people's rights or property or even their very lives. As people became civilized and developed villages and cities, the need for government became apparent. Over the centuries, it became a fixture of civilized life.

In recent decades, scholars have studied governmental and political processes and shaped a respected academic discipline. Political science is studied in great detail by students, researchers, professors, and others.

Areas of Study in Political Science

In its most basic terms, political science consists of the study of politics and government. Within this field, students and researchers tend to focus their attention on a few major areas. The following are descriptions of some primary areas of study in the field of political science.

National Politics

A major topic in political science is the study of national politics. In the United States, national politics consists of American or U.S. politics; in Canada, it involves the Canadian political system. The study of national politics typically concerns the philosophical foundations of the national-level government, constitutional development, and the various institutions within the government. Included in this area of study are the major branches of government and how they operate, as well as contemporary issues related to the electoral process, party politics, and government policies and practices at the national level.

Public Administration

Public administration deals with the practical aspects of managing government operations. It focuses on principles of administration such as planning, budgeting, and supervising. A common goal of public administration is to enhance the operating efficiency of public organizations.

Comparative Politics

Comparative politics evaluates political processes and governmental organizations relative to one another. This area of study can include the analysis of government at various levels. For example, the legislative process in different states may be compared, or the different ways local governments obtain tax revenues may be studied.

International Relations

No country exists in isolation. The interaction between countries is the basis for the study of international relations. Topics in this extensive area of study include trade agreements, mutual security treaties, economic exchanges, and other affairs among nations.

Other Areas of Study

Other areas of study range from constitutional law to the history of political parties. The University of Wisconsin has identified the following subfields of possible interest to political science majors:

- Political parties and voting behavior
- Bureaucracies and administrative procedure
- International politics and organization
- Executive politics and legislative behavior
- Political socialization and recruitment
- Community organization and urban politics

- Courts and the administration of justice
- Interest groups
- Intergovernmental relations
- Political personality
- Mass movements and revolutions
- Political philosophy
- Policy studies

Advantage of a Degree

A bachelor's degree is not always a quick ticket to a rewarding job. After all, more people are going to college now than ever before, and the current economy's shifting nature has created a great deal of uncertainty concerning careers.

At the same time, a bachelor's degree is almost always an asset, and with persistence most people who earn a college degree find it increases their occupational choices. Aside from its intrinsic value, a degree can be a major factor in landing a good job. After all, although more people are attending college, only about 20 percent of American adults hold a bachelor's degree or higher, according to the U.S. Census. That means four out of five adults in the United States lack a college degree. In seeking employment or in advancing on the job once you're employed, a degree can make the difference.

Political science graduates not only benefit from the general knowledge obtained in completing a liberal arts degree, but also acquire specialized knowledge about governmental systems. Some courses in this field cover broad areas of political philosophy, while others focus on more specific governmental practices. The combined result prepares political science majors to perform a wide range of tasks related to government, law, organizational management, and other areas.

An event sponsored by the University of Minnesota illustrates the diversity of careers open to political science majors. At a special career day, five former graduates of the political science program returned to campus and talked to students about their careers. The five included the Speaker of the Minnesota House of Representatives, a chief legislative aide to a U.S. senator, a graduate who went on to earn a law degree from Yale, a businesswoman who develops Web pages for private companies, and a graduate who works for a respected cultural organization.

According to University of Minnesota officials, many former graduates work in government. Substantial numbers have gone on to law school. Many others have used their liberal arts background to pursue employment in management, in the media, as lobbyists, and in other occupations. A similar story can be found for the graduates of almost any college or university offering a major in political science.

Many students who earn a bachelor's degree in political science go on to pursue a master's degree. This is a frequent choice of political science majors who hope to enhance their careers. The graduate degree may be in political science or a more specialized aspect of the field, such as international relations. Or it might be in a completely different field such as public administration, urban planning, business administration, finance, or communications.

Whether they go to graduate school or enter the workforce after completing a bachelor's degree, political science majors end up working in a wide range of career areas. Like any liberal arts field, political science, when combined with the other disciplines studied as part of the general education component of all bachelor's degrees, provides a solid foundation for understanding the world and for thinking critically. The tools learned in college, from reading and writing with skill to analyzing and understanding complex information, prepare students to adapt to a variety of workplace needs. In addition, the knowledge gained by political science students, such as how political systems operate and the basic processes of government, can be applied in a host of jobs. Preparation at the undergraduate level in political science can be the start of an exciting and productive career, from the lobbyist approaching a senator to the judge who interprets the constitutionality of a law introduced by the senator.

The following chapters cover some of the career paths that can be followed in this field. Listings are not exhaustive, but they should provide a good overview of some possibilities that await you. The following career paths are discussed:

1. Public service
2. Teaching
3. Law
4. Nonprofit management

These paths are offered as realistic suggestions, with the hope that they will stimulate your thinking about possible career directions. You will also be able to think of other options. With effort and creativity, you should be able to make a case for your political science degree in any number of job situations.

6

Path I: Public Service

Political science majors understand the importance of government. Much of their studies are based on the fact that without government in its various forms, our lives would be vastly different. In fact, it is no exaggeration to note that civilization in its present form would be impossible without government.

At its very basic levels, government can rely on work contributed by citizens. The original idea behind most state legislatures was that citizens would give a portion of their time to serve in the legislature, but this service would not be their profession. The idea of the part-time legislator is still alive today to some extent. But it has been greatly overshadowed by the growth of a different concept: the career public servant.

Today, millions of people earn their livelihoods as government employees. This category includes not only specialized areas such as teachers, military personnel, and others, but also a large number of managers and professional employees who conduct the work performed by government agencies.

Public service represents fertile ground for the political science major. Someone must provide the services demanded by the citizens of a highly structured society. In many cases that someone can be the holder of a political science degree.

Definition of the Career Path

"Public service" is a broad term. To begin to define it within the context of career planning, here are some basic facts about public service as a career path.

Public service jobs include jobs within various levels of government. The duties of many public service jobs require an understanding of government policies and regulations. Many involve direct work with government agencies. Some public service careers require very specific skills not normally attained by political science majors (for example, working as an engineer with the U.S. Army Corps of Engineers). Others involve a general understanding of politics, government, and related matters with which political science majors are quite familiar.

Public service jobs are attained in a variety of ways. Some, such as those of state legislators and members of Congress, require being elected by the public. Some public service jobs consist of positions appointed through a formal government process. For example, certain high-level jobs require being officially appointed by an executive such as a governor or by a legislative body. Others require going through a civil service process based on taking examinations or meeting other specific criteria. Still other jobs in public service involve an application process very similar to that of the business world. Instead of being elected or appointed by an official body, applicants go through an interview process and are selected by the supervisor for the position.

Almost all public service jobs involve working in a noncommercial, nonprofit role. Directly or indirectly, this means serving the public.

Possible Job Titles

The U.S. Department of Labor reports a wide range of job titles within the broad area of "government service." Look in the *Occupational Outlook Handbook* online (bls.gov/oco) or at your local library to find more. Just a few of the most typical titles include the following:

- Administrative officer
- Appeal referee or reviewer
- Budget analyst
- Business-enterprise officer
- Civil preparedness officer
- Claims adjudicator
- Commissioner, conservation of resources
- County agent
- County director, welfare
- Cultural affairs officer

- Customs inspector
- Deputy assessor
- Diplomatic officer
- Director of programs
- Economic development coordinator
- Election assistant or supervisor
- Insurance licensing supervisor
- Intelligence specialist
- Legislative aide or assistant
- Manager of city, county, or town
- Manager for health, safety, and environment programs
- Municipal services supervisor
- Occupational safety and health compliance officer
- Officer of housing management, identification, immigration, or information
- Prosecuting attorney
- Public affairs officer
- Public finance specialist
- Public utilities complaint analyst supervisor
- Public works commissioner
- Rehabilitation center manager
- Secretary of state
- Urban planner
- Welfare director

Possible Employers

Public service jobs can be found in a wide range of agencies and organizations. The federal government is made up of scores of agencies, departments, commissions, and bureaus. Each state also has its own elaborate governmental structure. City, town, and county governments, as well as regional consortia and other groups, also employ large numbers of personnel.

Here are some possible employers in the public service area. Many more could be listed; these are merely examples.

- Agency for International Development
- City governments
- County governments
- Environmental Protection Agency

- Executive Office of the President
- Federal government (Departments of Agriculture, Commerce, Education, Health and Human Services, State, etc.)
- Federal Trade Commission
- General Services Administration
- Military (Defense Logistics Agency; Departments of the Air Force, Army, Defense, Navy)
- National Aeronautics and Space Administration
- National Credit Union Administration
- National Science Foundation
- Nuclear Regulatory Commission
- Regional planning agencies
- State governments
- U.S. Information Agency
- U.S. Postal Service

Also, most states have several regional or metropolitan planning organizations. These groups conduct activities related to economic development, grant development, regional planning, and other functions. The following list includes just a few of these organizations:

- Delaware Valley Regional Planning Commission
- Green River Area Development District (Kentucky)
- Hampton Roads Planning District Commission (Virginia)
- Indian River County Metropolitan Planning Organization (Florida)
- Merrimack Valley Planning Commission (Massachusetts)
- Mid-Ohio Regional Planning Commission
- Northeastern Illinois Planning Commission
- Rhode Island State Planning Council
- South Alabama Regional Planning Commission
- Tampa Bay Regional Planning Council (Florida)

Representative Public Service Jobs

If you want to follow a career path directly related to your studies as a political science major, consider serving as a government official. Such jobs include positions in different branches of government at the local, state or provincial, and federal levels. Some, including state legislators and members of Congress, are elected positions. Others, such as state-level cabinet positions, are based on appointments from governors or other officials.

Executive positions involve the various responsibilities of managing government agencies or other governmental units. At the top of the list is the president of the United States. You may want to pursue this job, but openings are few and the competition is stiff! Other executive positions include state governors, lieutenant governors, city or town mayors, and county executives. In addition to highly visible elected executives, many positions involve administering the business of an agency, department, or other unit.

Town or City Manager. Most cities and towns (with the exception of very small communities) employ a professional manager. The person in this position is responsible for managing the day-to-day affairs of municipal government.

The responsibilities of this position vary widely. In a large city, much of the job involves supervising other managers and staff who take care of specific responsibilities ranging from economic development to collection of utility payments. In a small town, more "hands-on" work may be required because of a limited number of staff.

Typically, a city manager takes care of the everyday business of the city. He or she manages city employees, runs the municipal offices, and carries out the direction of the city council or other governing body.

Federal Agency Manager. Many governmental affairs are handled by agencies or similar bodies. For example, the Environmental Protection Agency monitors environmental concerns and implements laws passed by Congress in this area. The Department of Commerce focuses on business concerns. The State Department deals with foreign policy and relations with other nations.

These and countless other agencies and departments employ managers to implement policy, deal with the public, and provide general management oversight. Of course, duties vary widely. The secretary of state who gives a major speech to the United Nations and the junior assistant who clips newspaper articles from foreign newspapers work for the same agency and are both public servants.

State Agency Manager. While the federal government operates a labyrinth of agencies and departments, states and provinces also employ their own legions of managers, support staff, and other workers. Jobs of this type range from a state's director of public safety to the human resources managers who hire and evaluate state employees.

Legislative Assistant. Many public service jobs involve staff roles in support of government functions. For example, consider the role of the legislative assistant. Mention the prospect of a career as a legislator, and most people probably envision serving as a member of the U.S. Congress or Canada's Parliament. But this is actually a limited point of view. For every elected legislative position at the national level, there are scores of support roles. To a lesser degree this is also true at the state level. Many of these jobs require a solid understanding of the political process, and as such they represent job choices worth considering for political science majors.

The knowledge gained from studying political science applies directly to the career of a legislative assistant, including both federal and state positions. The U.S. Congress includes 100 senators and 435 members of the House of Representatives. Each of these elected officials employs a large staff of people assigned to a variety of support roles. In addition, congressional committees, major political parties, and other political organizations employ staff. Duties may include writing letters to constituents, developing draft legislation, conducting background research, planning election campaigns, or scheduling meetings with other legislators.

Elected Official. Of course, you can also seek elected office. Pick up a newspaper or watch televised news, and you will see plenty of information about the people representing you in government. If you aspire to become one of those representatives, a political science background can help get you started. Such roles include member of the House of Representatives, U.S. senator, state legislator, mayor, governor, attorney general, and others.

Training and Qualifications

A bachelor's degree is a good starting point in qualifying for a public service job. In some cases, a bachelor's is not required, but having a degree makes you more competitive.

With the federal government, holding a bachelor's degree makes you eligible for appointment at the GS-5 level (see section on earnings). You may be able to qualify for positions such as personnel specialist or budget analyst with a degree in any major, including political science.

After completing a bachelor's degree with a major in political science, you might want to pursue a master's degree. An advanced degree can be valuable both in landing new jobs and in advancing once you are employed. One advantage of graduate study is that in many cases you can study on a part-time basis while you work full time. Completing 36 credits for a master's degree is much more manageable than earning the 120 credits or more typically needed for a bachelor's degree.

One approach is to combine a bachelor's degree in political science with a master's degree in a different but related field. For example, a master's degree in urban planning can effectively complement a bachelor's in political science. Completion of the second degree can bring enhanced prospects for obtaining certain jobs. Typical positions include that of assistant town manager in a small town, assistant county administrator, or planning officer in a state or regional planning agency.

Titles of degree offerings vary. Examples include master of public administration, master of public policy, master of public affairs, master of public management, or master of public management and administration. Course offerings in public administration cover areas such as the following: economics, financial management, policy analysis, public sector institutions, legal procedures, organization management, and human resources management.

Many political science graduates find the master of public administration (M.P.A.) an attractive option. This degree can prepare you to work in diverse fields such as regional planning, city management, nonprofit management, environmental planning, or social services administration. According to the National Association of Schools of Public Affairs and Administration, over 6,000 graduate degrees in public administration are awarded annually. More than 200 colleges and universities offer programs in this field, and over 25,000 students are enrolled.

Another option is to seek a master's degree or higher in political science itself. Still another approach is to obtain a master of business administration (M.B.A.) or another degree that involves management.

Earnings

Those employed in public service jobs earn a wide range of salaries. Some people complain that in general, government jobs pay less than corresponding jobs in the private sector. But at the same time, government employees enjoy more job security. Not only are they protected by well-developed personnel policies, but their reality of life differs from that of most private businesses. After all, one company may go out of business or be acquired by another, but who's going to buy the government? Certainly government employees are vulnerable to cutbacks and other problems, but in general, they enjoy excellent job security as well as good benefits.

Salaries for federal government personnel may be established by a highly structured plan known as the General Schedule (GS) plan. Under this system, jobs are rated at fifteen different levels based on a combination of job demands and qualifications needed to fill the position. Specific salaries are attached to each level in a series of steps. Following are the 2003 pay ranges under the GS plan:

GS-5	$23,442–30,471
GS-6	$26,130–33,969
GS-7	$29,037–37,749
GS-8	$32,158–41,806
GS-9	$35,519–46,175
GS-10	$39,115–50,851
GS-11	$42,976–55,873
GS-12	$51,508–66,961
GS-13	$61,251–79,629
GS-14	$72,381–94,098
GS-15	$85,140–110,682

In determining actual pay, a number of factors may be considered. The government adjusts GS pay geographically, and when locality payments are included, pay rates within the continental United States may increase as much as 12 percent. Outside the continental United States, pay rates are 10 to 25 percent higher. In addition, some starting salaries in hard-to-fill fields are higher than the minimum. Experienced employees also tend to build up higher salaries the longer they stay with the job.

What if you have a college degree in political science but no directly related job experience? According to the U.S. Office of Personnel Management, you would start out at a GS-5 level. If you have maintained a B average or meet other academic credentials, you can start at GS-7. If you have a master's degree directly related to the job in question, you can qualify for a GS-9 rating.

Keep in mind that not all federal government jobs use the GS pay plan. For example, U.S. attorneys and judges have their own pay scales, as do members of Congress and those in a variety of other roles.

At the state and local levels, salaries vary tremendously from one state to the next or among different branches of government and different departments. To get an idea of salaries for jobs in your city or state, check ads for job openings or consult officials at government agencies in which you are interested.

Working Conditions

Because public service jobs cover so many areas, working conditions may vary markedly. In general, workers in this field enjoy comfortable working environments.

Typically, public service jobs involve a significant amount of office work. Office settings range from a tiny, single cubicle to an expansive office with plush furnishings. Often the physical setting is an indicator of authority and seniority, with senior executives enjoying larger and more impressive offices than those of more junior personnel. But this is by no means a standard practice. Office environments may vary depending on a number of factors: the age of the building in which an office is located, the historical allotment of office space in the organization, staffing trends resulting in increases or reductions in the demand for office space, and other considerations. Regardless of the size or furnishings of an office, it typically includes a few basics such as a desk, chair, telephone, and computer. Related work environments may include conference rooms, offices of coworkers, and large meeting rooms.

In addition, many public service jobs require work outside of the office setting, which can vary widely. A town manager or urban planner may spend time walking through old buildings designated for remodeling and use as part of a new industrial park. An employee of a U.S. embassy in another country may end up driving through a jungle to check on some American relief workers. A legislator may spend time visiting a constituent's farm one day and making a speech in the state capitol the next.

Strategies for Finding the Jobs

You can follow a number of strategies to identify job openings in public or government service. One approach is to work through professional associations. Whatever approach you use, take time to look at all the job listings, not just the entry-level ones for which you would be most qualified. Seeing the full range of available jobs gives you a good idea of what opportunities you might have later on in your career, and what positions you can ultimately attain with your political science degree.

The American Society for Public Administration (ASPA) has a membership of more than 10,000 people. Members include not only those employed in public service, but also teachers and students. Membership in this type of organization can be a valuable resource during the job search process. The ASPA's advantages include comprehensive national conferences, networking opportunities, continuing education, and other features. Of special interest to students, recent graduates, and other job seekers is the information ASPA provides about job opportunities. The organization maintains a master list of job openings around the country and makes this available online through its website.

A recent compilation of job listings included the following:

Employer	Position
U.S. General Accounting Office	Social science analyst
Broward County, Florida	Assistant county administrator
National Cancer Institute	Assistant director for financial management
Kent County, Michigan	Management intern
Clark County, Nevada	Human management intern
Federation for Community Planning	Senior budget analyst
City of Detroit	Director, planning and development department
Soros Foundation	Senior program officer for economic development

More information about the organization is available from the

**American Society for
 Public Administration**
1120 G St. NW,
 Suite 700
Washington, DC 20005
aspanet.org

For Canadians, a good source of job ads that include public service positions is

Canada Employment Weekly
21 New St.
Toronto, ON
Canada M5R 1P7
mediacorp2.com/cew

Each weekly issue of this publication lists hundreds of new position openings, including jobs in every province and territory of Canada.

The U.S. government's Office of Personnel Management lists job openings on a continuous basis. This includes job postings on its website (to access this information, simply key in "office of personnel management" while using any online search engine). In any given week, hundreds of job openings with the federal government are listed. A recent listing included openings for civil rights analyst, intelligence support analyst, social science analyst, policy analyst, and a variety of other jobs of potential interest to political science graduates.

A good source of job information at the state legislative level is the National Conference of State Legislatures. This organization, which serves legislators and legislative staff members from across the United States, lists job openings on its website. It also provides a wealth of information about legislative affairs that may be of interest to those considering employment in this area. For more information, contact

National Conference of State Legislatures
7700 E. First Pl.
Denver, CO 80230
hcls.org

A recent list of job openings in state legislatures included the following:

- Director, Wisconsin Integrated Legislative Information System Staff
- Economist, Arizona Joint Legislative Budget Committee
- Executive director, Tennessee General Assembly
- Executive director, Texas Legislative Reference Library
- Fiscal and policy analyst, California Legislative Analyst's Office
- Legislative information technology analyst and adviser, North Dakota Legislative Council
- Policy analyst, Florida Office of Program Policy Analysis and Government Accountability
- Staff coordinator, Washington State Senate Commerce and Labor Committee

Another source of information about government jobs is careersingovernment.com. This free online service identifies government job openings. For information, write to

Careers in Government
P.O. Box 1436
Agoura Hills, CA 91376
careersingovernment.com

Want to get involved in the heart of the political process? If so, one way is to seek employment with a major political party. In some cases, you may need to start out as a volunteer. The following are details for the Democratic and Republican parties:

**Democratic National
   Committee (DNC)**
430 S. Capitol St. SE
Washington, DC 20003
democrats.org
DNC campaign areas for possible work as a volunteer or staff member
   include presidential, U.S. Senate, U.S. House, state gubernatorial, state
   legislative, mayoral, and other state and local races.

**Republican National
   Committee (RNC)**
310 First St. SE
Washington, DC 20003
rnc.org
Some job titles of those who work for the RNC are chairman, cochairman,
   treasurer, chief counsel, executive director, communications director,
   press secretary, political director, finance director, member relations
   director, and administration director.

To find out about volunteer or job possibilities, contact the national head-quarters of the party in which you are interested. The national offices can also provide you with addresses and phone numbers of state offices for each respective political party.

Become More Knowledgeable About Public Issues

Your studies to date will have exposed you to an assortment of public policy issues. In preparing to seek positions in government or related areas, demonstrating familiarity with a broad range of issues will help your case. Some public policy issues you may want to demonstrate familiarity with include the following:

- Affirmative action and equal opportunity
- Capital punishment
- Censorship in electronic communications
- Drug use and related laws and policies
- Economic policy
- Education reform
- Federal versus local government responsibilities
- Government-sponsored health care
- International trade policy
- Political campaign finance
- Tax reform
- Welfare issues

Reading is one way to maintain a working knowledge of current affairs and topics related to politics and government. News magazines, newspapers, specialized magazines, and books all represent helpful sources of such information.

Other sources of valuable information include professional associations, both at the national (see the end of this chapter) and regional levels. An example of the latter is the Midwest Political Science Association (MPSA), which has nearly 3,000 members. It publishes the *American Journal of Political Science*, a leading journal for research in all major areas of political science. Every year the MPSA holds a three-day convention in Chicago, attended by more than 2,000 political scientists, students, and practitioners. More than 400 panels are conducted on all areas of political science. Political science students can use such forums as an excellent way not only to gain new knowledge, but also to make contacts and network with others in the field. Other organizations can be similarly helpful. See the list of such groups at the end of this chapter.

Try an Internship

If you want to gain valuable experience while still a student, consider serving as an intern. Internships in government agencies or other organizations provide excellent opportunities to supplement classroom learning. Some students serve as interns while still completing an undergraduate degree. Others seek internships as a part of master's or doctoral programs.

When you serve as an intern, you gain an inside look at what it's like to work in a given career field. You also make contacts that can prove valuable in the future for job reference and other purposes. In some cases, internships can lead directly to future employment with the agency you serve.

Typical duties for interns include the following examples provided by the National Association of Schools of Public Affairs and Administration:

- Conducting research and writing for think tanks
- Developing management information systems
- Coordinating economic and political surveys
- Researching and writing grant proposals
- Writing news releases and organizing public relations events
- Researching and designing project methodology
- Assisting in the implementation of development projects
- Conducting evaluations of ongoing projects

Steps Toward Employment

In its brochure "Political Science: The Ideal Liberal Arts Major," the American Political Science Association recommends a number of steps for undergraduate majors who will be seeking immediate employment. Among them are the following:

1. Consult professors and college placement counselors to obtain advice about job opportunities and especially about how your own skills and achievements can best be used.
2. Contact government agencies, corporations, newspapers, and professional associations to explore other job opportunities.
3. Prepare a résumé that highlights broad analytical and communication skills, internship and job experiences, and knowledge you've gained from political science courses.
4. Send your résumé to employers in which you're interested, and consult your placement office to schedule interviews with employers who will be visiting your campus.
5. Talk with people working in organizations that interest you and seek suggestions regarding possible employment.
6. Pursue an internship with an organization you find interesting, while still in college.

Remember, it's never too early to begin taking concrete steps that will support your job search. Keep in close touch with professors, counselors, and placement office staff, and maintain records that will help you in seeking employment.

Related Occupations

The skills that political science majors bring to jobs in government and public service are also valued in a number of related occupations. Here is a small sample of job areas that draw on similar skills:

- Association executive
- Corporate manager
- Editorial writer
- Educational administrator
- Government relations specialist for trade union
- Health agency manager
- Lobbyist
- Political pollster
- Speechwriter
- Volunteer coordinator

Professional Associations for Public Service Professionals

Academy of Political Science
475 Riverside Dr., Suite 1274
New York, NY 10015
jstor.org
Members/Purpose: Serves scholars and others interested in public policy.
Training: Offers issue-related conferences.
Journal/Publications: *Political Science Quarterly*; also publishes books on
   public policy issues.

American Federation of Government Employees
80 F St.
Washington, DC 20001
afge.org
Members/Purpose: Serves employees of the federal government in a variety
   of jobs; 250,000 members.
Training: Holds national meetings.
Journals/Publications: *Government Standard, AFGE Bulletin, The
   Equalizer.*

American Federation of State,
    County and Municipal Employees
1625 L St. NW
Washington, DC 20036
afscme.org
Members/Purpose: Membership includes more than 1.3 million
    government employees; serves as a union dealing with workplace issues
    of concern to government employees.
Training: Holds biennial meetings.
Journals/Publications: *AFSCME Leader, AFSCME Child Welfare Watch,*
    AFSCME Legislative Weekly Report.

American Political Science
    Association
1527 New Hampshire Ave. NW
Washington, DC 20036
apsanet.org
Members/Purpose: Members include more than 12,000 practitioners,
    teachers, and students.
Training: Offers conferences and educational materials.
Journals/Publications: *American Political Science Review, PS: Political*
    Science and Politics, Perspectives on Politics; a variety of other publications
    including brochure on "Earning a Ph.D. in Political Science."
Jobs: Lists job openings in its *Personnel Newsletter*; offers a job placement
    service.

Canadian Political Science
    Association
204 Dalhousie St.
Ottawa, ON
Canada K1N 7E4
cpsa-acsp.ca
Members/Purpose: Members include more than 1,100 faculty from
    Canadian colleges and universities, plus politicians and public servants.
    Supports understanding of the field of political science.
Training: Conference every year.
Journals/Publications: *Canadian Journal of Political Science, CPSA Bulletin,*
    Canadian Public Policy, Careers for Political Scientists.
Jobs: Lists job openings in its bulletin and online.

**Inter-University Consortium for
Political and Social Research**
P.O. Box 1248
Ann Arbor, MI 48106
icpsr.umich.edu
Members/Purpose: Supports research in the social sciences, including
political science.
Training: Conference every other year.
Journal/Publication: *ICPSR Bulletin.*

**National Association of Schools of Public Affairs
and Administration**
1120 G St. NW
Washington, DC 20005
naspaa.org
Members/Purpose: More than 200 university programs in public affairs
and administration and more than 35 associate members. Accredits
master's degree programs in public affairs and administration. Promotes
excellence in public service education.
Training: Annual conference.
Journals/Publications: *Public Enterprise* newsletter, *Journal of Public Affairs
Education*; special papers, reports, and monographs.

**National Conference of
State Legislatures**
7700 E. First Pl.
Denver, CO 80230
or
44 N. Capitol St. NW
Washington, DC 20001
ncsl.org
Members/Purpose: Serves legislators and legislative staff members from the
fifty states; provides research, publications, consulting services, and
educational opportunities.
Training: Sponsors annual meeting; also holds about twenty seminars and
conferences yearly.
Journals/Publications: *State Legislatures* magazine, various reports on
legislative matters; also offers an online directory of state legislatures.
Jobs: Lists job openings around the country on its website.

Southern Political Science Association
P.O. Box 8101
2288 Carroll Bldg.
Georgia Southern University
Statesboro, GA 30460
www2.gasou.edu/spsa
Members/Purpose: Serves faculty, students, and others interested in the field.
Training: Sponsors conferences.
Journal/Publications: *The Journal of Politics.*

7

Path 2: Teaching

As a student of political science, you have developed an understanding of the basic processes of government and the various aspects of politics. But just how did you acquire this knowledge? In large part it was due to the work of teachers. From your first course in government as a middle or high school student to the varied courses you have taken as a college political science major, teachers have played a key role in your intellectual development.

As you plan ahead, one option is for you to take on the instructional role. After all, a continuing demand exists for people with the right credentials and the appropriate talents to teach political science or related subjects.

Teachers teach. That sounds simple, but in reality they do much more than deliver lectures. Here are just some of the responsibilities of teachers and professors:

- Using various teaching methods to instruct students
- Employing audiovisual aids to supplement presentations
- Preparing course objectives and outlines
- Assigning readings, papers, and other student work
- Creating and administering tests
- Evaluating student work and assigning grades
- Advising students
- Participating in committees and professional assignments
- Performing public or community service
- Reviewing potential textbooks and instructional support materials
- Revising and updating curricula
- Participating in professional development functions
- Maintaining course and student records
- Reading and keeping current in the discipline

For those who teach political science at the college level or government at the middle or high school level, responsibilities are intertwined with the continued study of current events. Political science is an active, constantly changing discipline and a fascinating area to teach.

Certainly, teaching is not for everyone. But if you are a good communicator and feel you can share your knowledge effectively with others, this career path is worth considering.

Definition of the Career Path

Political science is a respected academic discipline taught widely in colleges and universities. Students who study political science include both those who choose to major or minor in the field and those who take such classes as a part of their general studies requirements or as electives.

Middle schools and high schools frequently require classes in civics, American government, and related areas. Many states and school districts consider it vital that every student take at least one such course to promote better citizenship.

A career focus closely related to teaching is educational administration. Every school and college has administrators who manage its academic affairs, as well as those in areas ranging from executive management to administrative support.

Possible Job Titles

The importance of the political science field has meant a continuing demand for men and women qualified to teach it. As a result, teaching political science or related subjects is a promising career path for those with the right inclinations. The following are some job titles in this career path:

- Teacher, middle school (civics, social studies)
- Teacher, high school (civics, American government, social science)
- Adjunct faculty member
- Graduate teaching assistant
- Lecturer
- Instructor of political science
- Assistant professor of political science or public administration
- Associate professor of political science or urban studies
- Professor of political science

Possible Employers

If you want to teach political science or related subjects, you can go in any of several directions. One approach is to become a professor at a four-year college or university. An alternative is to join the faculty of a community, junior, or technical college. Still another direction is to become a middle school or high school teacher.

Four-Year Colleges and Universities

Teaching at the university or four-year college level is a primary goal of many students who major in political science. Almost every college and university offers courses in political science, so a continuing demand exists for faculty with the appropriate training and credentials to teach those courses.

A variety of four-year colleges and universities operate throughout the United States and Canada, including major universities, medium-sized institutions, and small colleges, both public and private. Although not all offer undergraduate majors in political science, the majority do, and some also offer master's or doctoral level programs.

At the university level, most political science faculty function in two different ways. First, they teach general courses such as "Introduction to Political Science." Second, they teach, conduct research, and publish in a specialized area of their interest. Here are some as identified by the American Political Science Association:

- African-American politics
- American government and politics
- Comparative politics
- Country/area politics (Latin American politics, European politics, etc.)
- Electoral behavior and public opinion
- International organizations and law
- International relations and world politics
- International security and arms control
- Legislative politics
- Methodology
- Political communication
- Political parties and interest groups
- Political philosophy
- Political psychology and socialization
- Politics and history
- Presidential and executive politics

- Public administration
- Public law and judicial politics
- Public policy
- Urban and ethnic politics
- Women and politics

In recent years, the college teaching profession has taken a great deal of criticism. Some critics contend that professors are under-worked and enjoy too many privileges compared to other workers in North American society.

While this may be true of some poorly motivated faculty, teaching at the college level is actually quite demanding. Not only must professors give lectures and perform other teaching duties, but they are also expected to conduct research, write articles and books, and perform public service, among other duties. In addition, they advise students, serve on committees, develop and refine courses, and spend many hours simply keeping up in their fields.

Even though this life can be challenging, it is considered by many as one of the most desirable careers available. College faculty members enjoy shorter work years, interesting work environments, and hours that usually vary from the nine-to-five routines of much of the business world. At most schools, faculty can qualify for tenure, which provides an unsurpassed measure of job security. All in all, teaching political science in a university or four-year college can be a great career path.

Two-Year Colleges

Even though they may not offer majors in the subject, most community, junior, and technical colleges offer courses in political science. Students who plan to transfer to four-year schools can take these courses as part of their associate degree program. Other students also may take a political science course or two to meet general studies requirements or as electives. The result is a demand for faculty to teach political science courses in the two-year college setting.

Sometimes, community college faculty members specialize in political science and teach only in that discipline. In other instances, especially in smaller schools, they teach a second discipline (such as history) or some other field in the social sciences. Generally this means having completed sufficient courses at the graduate level in both disciplines to meet accrediting agency requirements. In any case, teaching in two-year colleges is a viable career option for political science majors willing to earn at least a master's degree.

The biggest difference in community college teaching and other college instruction is the course load. In universities, faculty may teach as few as two or three courses per semester. In two-year colleges, it's more typical to teach five courses per semester. This means community college faculty spend more time in class than their university counterparts. They also tend to devote correspondingly more time in grading papers, preparing lectures, and other instructional tasks. Also, faculty in two-year schools often spend significant amounts of time advising students, serving on college committees, and performing other duties. They do all this without the help of graduate students or teaching assistants.

All this activity leaves little time for research or writing. But unlike four-year college or university faculty, those teaching in two-year colleges are not generally expected to make research and writing a routine part of their jobs. They are viewed as professional teachers rather than researchers.

High School

Almost every high school offers courses in civics, government, or related areas. Therefore, teaching high school has real job potential for those willing to obtain the right credentials and who can teach kids effectively.

Teaching in high school can be very different from teaching at the college level. In addition to time spent on in-class teaching, grading papers, and performing related instructional work, working as a high school government or civics teacher can mean performing the following tasks:

- Serving as an adviser to a student club or organization
- Performing hall or bus duty
- Eating lunch with students and supervising their behavior
- Disciplining unruly students
- Driving students to extracurricular activities (such as a model United Nations session)
- Chaperoning at a dance
- Meeting with parents on a routine basis
- Meeting with parents when a student is experiencing special problems
- Serving on an accreditation self-study team
- Serving on a committee to hire a new teacher or administrator
- Ordering textbooks, software, or supplies
- Coordinating mock elections

Following is a list of skills high school teachers need for success (adapted from requirements at Virginia's Radford University):

- Planning, implementing, and evaluating instruction
- Managing classroom and administrative tasks
- Collecting and interpreting student data

- Promoting students' cognitive, psychomotor, and socioaffective development
- Providing for individual and cultural differences
- Applying knowledge of social forces that affect professional responsibility in a global society
- Working with others in conducting professional tasks and in pursuing professional development
- Applying a breadth and depth of knowledge of the teaching specialty area

Educational Administration

Typically, administrative personnel in the educational setting start out as teachers and then progress to administrative roles. In the middle school or high school setting, a teacher interested in administrative work might take on a role such as assistant principal. This may require completion of additional classes or a degree in educational administration, coupled with sufficient teaching experience. After spending some time as an assistant principal, an administrator might move on to a principal's position, and from there to a central office position such as curriculum coordinator, director of pupil services, or assistant superintendent of schools. A relatively few administrators might eventually assume top-level roles such as superintendent of schools or state-level positions such as state superintendent of schools.

At the college level, a professor of political science might take on the role of department chairperson. In higher education, specific training in administration is not necessarily required. Quite often faculty members learn "on the job" once they are appointed to administrative positions, although some who aspire to administrative jobs complete master's or doctoral degrees in administrative or management fields. Some faculty take on administrative roles only temporarily and then return to teaching. Others become career administrators. They may go on to hold positions such as dean, vice president, or college president.

Training and Qualifications

A bachelor's degree is just the starting point for a career in higher education. At the minimum, a master's degree is necessary, and many positions require a doctorate. Completing teacher education courses is not necessary. Instead, the minimum requirement is a master's degree earned in political science or a master's degree in another field with a significant number of graduate courses in political science. Exact requirements for minimum credentials vary with the type of institution and the demands of regional agencies that accredit colleges and universities. The Southern Association of Colleges and Schools, for example, stipulates that all faculty teaching college-level political science courses hold, as a minimum, a master's degree with at least eighteen graduate hours in political science. Many community college faculty hold teaching positions with this level of preparation, although some also hold doctorates.

In most four-year colleges and universities, it is generally expected that faculty hold a doctoral degree. Even if not an absolute requirement, this becomes a matter of practicality in the job search process (if fifty candidates apply for a position and thirty-five have doctorates, the chances of landing that job with only a master's degree are understandably limited).

If you want to earn a doctorate, you will need dedication and persistence. A doctoral degree requires several years of full-time study beyond the bachelor's degree (there is no specific time frame; duration varies). More than just taking additional classes of the same type you completed as an undergraduate, earning a doctorate also requires mastering research methodologies and learning to function as an independent researcher.

An excellent brochure is available to guide you on this subject. "Earning a Ph.D. in Political Science" is free on request from

American Political Science Association
1527 New Hampshire Ave. NW
Washington, DC 20036
apsanet.org

The Grad School Game
If you're thinking about going on to graduate school and studying political science, here are some strategies to get you there.

Earn Good Grades. Obviously, the higher your grades, the better. If you're still in school but your grades could be better, it's not too late. Most graduate schools will look more closely at the last two years of college and at your major area of study. If you're already out of school, consider taking a few additional political science courses at the bachelor's level and strive for the best possible grades, or do the same thing as a part-time or provisional student at the master's level.

Take the Graduate Record Examination (GRE). This is a fairly standard requirement for graduate school admission. The American Political Science Association recommends that if your score is not in the 80th or 90th percentile, you should consider retaking the exam. In this case, putting in some advance studying or investing in a test preparation class can be worthwhile. Also, keep in mind that good grades or other factors can sometimes help offset mediocre scores.

Line Up Good Sources for Letters of Recommendation. Professors who know your work will usually be glad to write recommendation letters. Be sure to contact faculty with sufficient lead time to avoid potential problems in meeting deadlines. Also, offer to provide background information that will make writing a letter easier, such as a list of political science courses you have taken or the exact dates and names of courses taken under that particular professor.

Check Around. Don't just set your sights on one school, but take some time to check out others. According to the American Political Science Association, over 130 colleges and universities in the United States offer doctoral degrees in political science. Others offer master's level programs. With so many different schools to choose from, the odds are on your side of finding at least one school that matches your particular interests and abilities.

Opportunities for Minorities

If you are a minority student, you should be aware of some special opportunities available to you. Many universities offer scholarship and fellowship programs that provide support for graduate study as well as special programs to promote diversity.

The American Political Science Association offers two programs designed to identify and provide assistance to minorities. First, the Minority Fellows Program is a fellowship designed to increase the number of minority Ph.D.'s in political science. It also encourages colleges and universities to provide financial assistance to minority students. Second, the Ralph Bunche Summer Institute is a five-week program offered every year that introduces minority American students to the world of graduate study and encourages them to pursue doctoral degrees.

For details about these programs, contact

American Political Science
    Association
1527 New Hampshire Ave. NW
Washington, DC 20036
apsanet.org

Teaching High School

To prepare for teaching at the high school level, a political science major must be combined with courses designed to prepare students to become certified as teachers. Details of this process vary in different states and among different colleges and universities. Generally, this involves completing courses in teacher education, successfully completing a student teaching experience, and passing standardized examinations.

The most common standard for teaching at the high school level is a bachelor's degree plus certification or licensure to teach. The latter is usually obtained by taking education courses and passing a comprehensive examination required by the state board of education or equivalent body in the state where you live or plan to teach.

At one time, preparing to teach meant majoring in education (sometimes called teacher education) while also taking courses in subjects you planned to teach. Nowadays, many colleges and universities follow a different model where you major in the specific discipline of your interest and also take a selection of education courses, including student teaching.

If you are a political science major, you can qualify to teach at the high school level by completing all the requirements for a degree in political science, plus completing the education courses required by your college and state. Ideally, you do this concurrently with your other studies. If you are near the end of your bachelor's degree, or have already completed it, and decide to pursue a secondary teaching career, you will need to go back and complete these education requirements.

An alternative to this approach offered by some colleges is to complete a special program that brings you in compliance with the necessary requirements. Concordia University in Michigan offers a post-baccalaureate teacher certification program, for example. This program allows bachelor's degree holders to become certified teachers. Another approach is to earn a master's degree in education, completing teacher certification requirements in the process.

Earnings

According to the College and University Personnel Association (CUPA), college and university professors in four-year schools earned average salaries of $60,000–61,000 in 2001–2002.

The U.S. Department of Labor reported that in 2000, median annual earnings of postsecondary teachers were $46,330, with the middle 50 percent earning between $32,270 and $66,460. The highest 10 percent earned more than $87,850. For each subsequent year, an increase of 2 to 5 percent would be a reasonable estimate.

Keep in mind that faculty salaries vary according to many factors, including credentials, faculty rank, geographic area, longevity, and type or level of institution.

Do secondary-school teachers make good salaries? That depends on who you ask. Many teachers complain about unattractive salaries, and they have a point. Compared to earnings of many other professionals, teacher pay is low. But at the same time, salaries are not really that bad. In an era when many college graduates find it difficult to find jobs following graduation, a job in teaching offers solid if unspectacular pay, as well as good benefits such as health insurance and retirement plans.

In addition, teachers enjoy more time off than almost any other workers. Most work under nine- or ten-month contracts, providing for significant time off in the summer as well as during holidays. Many teachers use this time to pursue part-time jobs, run their own businesses, or otherwise supplement their income. They may also take advantage of this time to attend graduate school, travel, or pursue other personal interests.

Salary levels for teachers are usually determined at the local level. Most school districts follow a strict salary schedule based on education and years spent on the job. According to the National Education Association, average salaries of public schoolteachers in 2001–2002 were as follows:

California	$53,870
Connecticut	$53,551
New York	$52,040
Michigan	$52,037
New Jersey	$51,186
Pennsylvania	$50,599
Illinois	$50,000
Rhode Island	$49,758
Alaska	$49,418
Massachusetts	$49,054
Delaware	$48,363
District of Columbia	$47,049
Maryland	$46,200
Oregon	$46,039
Nevada	$44,738
Indiana	$44,195

Georgia	$44,073
Ohio	$44,029
Washington	$43,474
Minnesota	$43,330
Hawaii	$42,615
Wisconsin	$42,232
North Carolina	$41,991
Virginia	$41,262
Colorado	$40,222
Arizona	$39,973
Florida	$39,275
Alabama	$39,268
Vermont	$39,240
Texas	$39,232
South Carolina	$38,943
New Hampshire	$38,911
Tennessee	$38,554
Iowa	$38,230
Missouri	$37,904
Kentucky	$37,847
Wyoming	$37,841
Idaho	$37,482
Utah	$37,414
Maine	$37,300
Arkansas	$37,140
West Virginia	$36,751
Kansas	$36,673
New Mexico	$36,440
Nebraska	$36,236
Oklahoma	$34,744
Louisiana	$34,505
Montana	$34,379
Mississippi	$32,800
North Dakota	$31,709
South Dakota	$31,295

Salaries for teachers in private high schools tend to be somewhat lower than for public schoolteachers, although actual salaries vary from one school to the next.

Strategies for Finding the Jobs

Finding a teaching job requires an aggressive approach. This is especially true at the college level. Although jobs can be found, chances are that for any given opening, a significant number of candidates will apply. So to be successful, you must take advantage of the various sources of information about job openings.

College Teaching Jobs

Professional organizations provide a great avenue for locating job openings and for the networking that can help lead to successfully obtaining a position.

For example, the American Political Science Association is a solid source of job information. In fact, it maintains a listing of all job openings at the assistant professor and associate professor level in the United States. To access this information, check out the organization's website or write to the address provided on page 100. The Canadian Political Science Association (CPSA) provides similar assistance. Job notices are posted in its bulletin, and conferences and meetings provide opportunities for networking. See page 90 for the CPSA address. Other organizations, both at the national and regional level, can also be helpful in the job search process.

Another great source of information is the National Center for Education Statistics' IPEDS College Opportunities On-Line (nces.ed.gov/ipeds/cool), a government-maintained website providing links to over 9,000 colleges, universities, and other post-secondary institutions in the United States. You can use this site to locate colleges and universities offering programs in political science or related areas. The site allows you to search not only by a specific program or degree offering, but also by location. Once you enter your chosen search parameters and look over the results, you can then obtain additional information by visiting the websites of individual schools, or by writing or calling for more information.

Virtually all colleges now maintain websites offering a wide variety of information, including details about job openings. Look under headings such as "Employment Opportunities," "Job Openings," or "Human Resources" to identify faculty position openings at any school in which you might be interested.

Graduate school professors and university placement offices can also be helpful in the job search process. Their assistance can be useful in obtaining letters of recommendation, locating part-time or temporary teaching positions, and networking with potential employers.

Various publications list job openings in teaching and related areas. Taking the time to peruse such publications can pay off handsomely, at least in terms of finding out about available jobs.

The Chronicle of Higher Education. In identifying teaching opportunities at the college level, a first-rate source of information is the *Chronicle of Higher Education*. This publication includes extensive job listings in every issue. In fact, a typical issue may include hundreds of job openings in colleges throughout the United States and a number in other countries, including several in political science.

For example, one issue included the following ad for a college teaching job at Ball State University in Indiana:

The Department of Political Science seeks to fill a tenure-track appointment at the Assistant or Associate Professor level in public policy and public administration beginning August 22. Responsibilities include teaching graduate courses in the M.P.A. program, including public policy and public administration, and additional graduate and undergraduate courses in the candidate's area of specialization. The candidate will complement a 14-person department offering M.A. and M.P.A. degrees.

Minimum qualifications: earned Ph.D. in political science with a major concentration in public policy and public administration. Preferred qualifications: record of scholarly activity; instruction at the college level.

To apply, submit letter of application describing research interests and courses prepared to teach, curriculum vitae, official transcripts, teaching evaluations if available, and three letters of recommendation.

In addition to job listings, the *Chronicle* publishes a wide variety of information about higher education, including book reviews, editorials, and in-depth stories about current issues in education, research trends, education financing, professional issues, and other matters. For those who work in higher education or who aspire to employment in academe, the *Chronicle* provides fascinating reading and helpful background.

The *Chronicle of Higher Education* is published on a weekly basis except for the third week in August and the last two weeks of December. It is available in college and university libraries and some public libraries, as well as through subscription at the following address:

Chronicle of Higher Education
1255 23rd St. NW
Washington, DC 20037
chronicle.com

Community College Week. This publication caters specifically to employees at two-year colleges. It includes a section of classified ads for positions at various institutions. Although job listings are not as extensive as those in the *Chronicle of Higher Education,* they are valuable for those interested in pursuing teaching jobs in community, junior, or technical colleges.

To obtain a copy or subscribe, write to

Community College Week
10520 Warwick Ave., Suite B-8
Fairfax, VA 22030-3136
ccweek.com

High School and Middle School Teaching Jobs
Seeking a teaching position in a middle school or high school usually involves more of a local emphasis than does the college hiring process. While most colleges advertise regionally or nationally for full-time vacancies, the typical school district relies more on local or statewide advertising. Thus a good way to learn about openings is to consult the want-ad sections of newspapers.

An increasingly productive way to seek out teaching jobs is to use the Internet. Many school districts now post information about their schools, including details about job openings, on the Internet. In addition, some websites specialize in providing job-related information for educators and potential education personnel (note: a fee is often charged). Examples include the following:

- K-12jobs.com (k12jobs.com). This site serves both employers and job seekers at the preschool and elementary, middle, and high school levels.
- Teacherjobs.com (teacherjobs.com) is a site maintained by Educational Placement Service (EPS), which bills itself as the largest placement service in the United States. This firm helps place educators in public, private, and parochial schools at the elementary, secondary, and college levels. More details are available at the website or at the company's headquarters: Educational Placement Service, 90 S. Cascade, Suite 1110, Colorado Springs, CO 80903.

- Educationjobs.com (educationjobs.com). This site provides a directory with links to more than 10,000 teaching, administrative, and coaching jobs.

Other similar services may be available for your area or for states or regions in which you're interested. To locate them, just use any Internet search engine and seek out "teaching jobs" or similar identifiers.

Another strategy is to contact school districts directly. Ask for a list of any anticipated job openings, and submit a résumé or application. Or you can even send your résumé and cover letter to all of the schools or school districts in which you would like to teach. Be sure to mention in your cover letter the types of courses and positions you are interested in, and the schools will keep your résumé on file.

Some prospective teachers use substitute teaching as a way to get started. Often, those who have served as substitutes become a "known quantity" and may gain an edge when full-time positions become available.

A helpful source of job-related information is the *Job Search Handbook for Educators*. It provides a variety of tips on pursuing jobs in education. For information, contact

Job Search Handbook for Educators
American Association for
   Employment in Education
3040 Riverside Dr., Suite 125
Columbus, OH 43221-2550
aaee.org

Related Occupations

Political science can also lead to other career paths related to teaching. The skills used in the classroom are not unlike those used in a number of other occupations. Consider the following job titles as a beginning list. Then investigate these and other positions that tap into the skill base you have already developed.

- Corporate trainer
- Educational consultant
- Human resources professional
- Policy analyst

- Public affairs specialist
- Researcher
- Sales representative, educational publishing company
- Textbook editor
- Textbook writer
- Tutor

Professional Associations for Teachers, Professors, and Related Professionals

American Association of Behavioral and Social Scientists (AABSS)
Box 27F, University of Tampa
401 W. Kennedy Blvd.
Tampa, FL 33606
aabss.org
Members/Purpose: Provides a professional network for behavioral and social scientists and related professionals.
Training: Annual meeting.
Journals/Publications: *AABSS Perspectives, AABSS Journal.*

American Association of University Professors
1012 14th St. NW, Suite 500
Washington, DC 20005
aaup.org
Members/Purpose: Serves college and university faculty.
Training: Meetings and other conferences.
Journal/Publications: *Academe*; also publishes newsletters and annual faculty salary report.

National Council for the Social Studies
8555 16th St., Suite 500
Silver Spring, MD 20910
ncss.org
Members/Purpose: Members include more than 20,000 teachers of social studies, including teachers of civics, political science, and other fields.
Training: Annual conference.
Journals/Publications: *Social Education, Middle Level Learning, Social Studies and the Young Learner, The Social Studies Professional.*

National Education Association
1201 16th St. NW
Washington, DC 20036
nea.org
Members/Purpose: Professional organization advancing the cause of public education; approximately 2.7 million members represent all areas of education from preschool to graduate programs.
Training: Meetings and conferences.
Journals/Publications: *NEA Today, Higher Education Advocate, Tomorrow's Teachers, Thought and Action.*

Social Science Research Council
810 7th Ave.
New York, NY 10019
ssrc.org
Members/Purpose: Members are social scientists in a variety of fields, including political scientists and faculty; promotes interdisciplinary research.
Journal/Publications: *Items & Issues;* working papers.

8

Path 3: Law

A common goal of political science students is to go on to law school and then enter the legal profession. Many successful attorneys started out by completing an undergraduate major or minor in political science.

The practice of law is an old and well-established profession. In the twenty-first century, it remains one of the most attractive of all professional paths. Most attorneys complete interesting work, earn excellent incomes, and enjoy a high level of prestige.

Students who want to become lawyers need not major in any one discipline while studying as undergraduates. In fact, "prelaw" majors can study in virtually any liberal arts field, including some outside the traditional arts and sciences, and still go on to law school. It is in law school that prospective attorneys acquire the specific knowledge and skills they will need to become practicing lawyers.

At the same time, many students who aspire to become lawyers major in political science. A natural connection exists between the study of political science and the study of law. Since political science covers government and politics, and attorneys deal with the interpretation of laws promulgated by government, those who study and understand political science may put themselves in a favorable position for understanding the legal system and the ways attorneys work within it.

Definition of the Career Path

Sometimes they're called attorneys. Other times they're dubbed lawyers. In either case, these professionals act as advocates and advisers. They represent opposing parties in court and advise clients about legal matters. In the process, lawyers interpret the law and apply it to business and personal affairs affecting their clients.

Conducting research is a major part of an attorney's job. This involves studying laws and judicial decisions that may apply to the particular circumstances of a given case. In the past, this meant consulting law books, journals, and other written records. While that is still a part of the job today, using computers to conduct research is an increasingly important part of a lawyer's work.

Lawyers also spend a great deal of their time communicating. They write and edit documents, present oral information, and interview clients and witnesses.

While the general title for this occupation is lawyer or attorney, titles may also be more specific depending on the area of specialization. These areas can be as diverse as working for corporations or environmental agencies, and include admiralty, criminal, insurance, labor, patent, and real estate law.

Some lawyers, especially those operating their own practices or working in small firms, practice in a variety of areas. But many lawyers specialize. Law is a complex subject requiring a great deal of in-depth knowledge not only to begin practicing in the first place, but also to maintain ongoing competency. For this reason, and for business purposes such as attracting specific types of clients, it is often more practical to focus on one or two areas.

To learn more about law, read publications about the subject. Several books and magazines of interest are listed at the end of this book. Also, an excellent source of information for attorneys working on their own or those working in small firms is *Lawyers Weekly*. This publication includes a national version (*Lawyers Weekly USA*) as well as state-specific versions for Massachusetts, Michigan, Maine, North Carolina, Ohio, Rhode Island, and Virginia. For information, contact

Lawyers Weekly
41 West St.
Boston, MA 02111
lawyersweekly.com

Possible Employers

Some attorneys are self-employed, operating their own law practices. Others work for law firms, government agencies, corporations, or other organizations. Some possible employers of lawyers follow:

- Banks
- City governments
- Colleges
- County governments
- Insurance companies
- Interest groups
- Manufacturing firms
- Private law firms
- Professional associations
- Real estate agencies
- Religious organizations
- State agencies
- U.S. Department of Defense
- U.S. Department of Justice
- U.S. Treasury Department

Training and Qualifications

Becoming a lawyer is possible only after intense training. Most students who pursue law first earn a bachelor's degree and then complete three years of law school. Then they take the bar exam required in their state and also complete an ethics examination.

Applying to Law School
If you're a political science major or recent graduate and decide to try for a legal career, the first step is applying for admission to law school.

Most law schools require the following from applicants:

1. A completed application for admission. This is available on request from any law school.
2. An application fee. The amount varies, but $50 is typical. Some schools require an additional confirmation deposit from accepted candidates.
3. Letters of recommendation. Usually, these are from professors who know your work.
4. Transcripts of your college credits and grades. Initially, transcript details can be forwarded through the Law School Data Assembly Service (LSDAS), a special clearinghouse that provides this service. After acceptance, official copies of transcripts will be required.

5. Test scores. Your scores from the Law School Admission Test (LSAT) will be a necessary part of the application package (see the following section for more details).

For more information about applying to law school, write to

American Bar Association
750 N. Lake Shore Dr.
Chicago, IL 60611
abanet.org

A good source of information about Canadian law schools is Jurist Canada, a website providing links to Canadian law schools, websites for individual law courses, and more. Check it out at jurist.law.utoronto.ca under the heading of "Studying Law."

If you want to go to law school, you'll have to take the Law School Admission Test (LSAT). There's almost no getting around it. Most law schools in the United States and Canada require prospective students to take this test.

Sitting for the LSAT can be challenging, but the experience is not all that different from taking the SAT or any other standardized test you took before enrolling in college. The exam is a half-day test consisting of multiple-choice questions broken up into five sections of 35 minutes each, plus a half-hour writing sample. To prepare for the LSAT, you may want to purchase a test preparation book or check one out from a library. Or you may consider enrolling in a review course or seminar.

Scores range from 120 to 180, with the latter being the highest score. The writing sample is not scored but is sent on to the schools you apply to. The LSAT measures the following thinking skills:

- Reading and comprehending complex texts with accuracy and insight
- Organizing and managing information, and drawing reasonable inferences from it
- Reasoning critically
- Analyzing and evaluating the reasoning and arguments of others

Studying Law

Once you start law school, you will be immersed in a thorough and demanding curriculum. In most cases, completing a Juris Doctor degree (the typical degree pursued by most law students) requires three years of full-time study. The actual time varies by school, type of degree, and whether you attend part-time, which is an option offered at some law schools.

The courses taken to earn a law degree vary. A typical pattern is to take a fairly rigid schedule of courses the first year; thereafter, more flexibility allows some choice of courses based on personal interests and specialization in specific areas of law.

At the Vanderbilt University Law School in Nashville, Tennessee, in addition to their program requirements, students complete a number of courses selected from a wide variety of choices, including the following:

- Administrative Law
- Advanced Environmental Law
- Advanced Evidence and Trial Advocacy
- Advanced Legal Research
- Advanced Topics in Labor and Employment Law Seminar
- Advanced Torts
- American Legal History
- Bioethics and the Law
- Children and the Law Seminar
- Complex Litigation
- Conflict of Laws
- Constitutional Law of U.S. Foreign Relations
- Consumer Credit Protection
- Copyright
- Criminal Practice and Procedure
- Current Constitutional Issues
- Employment Discrimination Law
- Environmental Law
- European Legal Institutions
- Family Law
- Federal Courts and the Federal System
- Health Law and Policy
- International and Comparative Business
- Introduction to Federal Income Taxation of Individuals
- Introduction to Legal Research and Scholarly Writing in the United States
- Labor Relations Law
- Local Government Law
- Patents, Trademarks, and Know-How
- Professional and Ethical Considerations in Corporate Practice
- Public Education Law
- Race and the Law
- Securities Regulation

- Social Choice, Fairness, and the Law
- Sports Law
- Trade and Wealth Law Seminar
- White Collar Crime
- Wills and Trusts

For the specific curriculum offered by any law school, check its website or printed course catalog.

Earnings

Lawyers are generally well paid. In fact, the attractive earnings potential for a career in law is one of the main incentives for many people who pursue this field.

Like any complex field, salaries actually vary quite widely. Senior partners in successful law firms or lawyers holding high-level corporate positions may earn several hundred thousand dollars a year, or even more. At the other extreme, a newly hired associate in a small firm may be paid $35,000 or $40,000 annually. According to the National Association of Law Placement, median salaries in 2002 for first-year associates were $53,300 in firms of 2 to 25 attorneys, and $118,000 in firms employing 500 or more attorneys.

In government jobs (such as U.S. attorneys and assistant attorneys) salary ranges follow strict guidelines established by the government. In the private sector, salaries have more room for difference. Law firms and corporations may establish their own salary levels based on previous company policy and current market conditions. These salary levels may vary quite widely. Obviously, a Chicago firm with 150 lawyers will have greater resources than a two-person law firm in a small Mississippi town. Also, some attorneys prefer to start their own practices. In this case, earnings will depend entirely on the success of the firm, as with any small business.

Working Conditions

Attorneys work in courtrooms, right? They sit at tables with their clients or walk around performing for the judge or jury like characters from innumerable movies and television shows.

Well, that is true some of the time, for some lawyers. But attorneys spend a great deal of time in settings outside of courtrooms. And some never set foot in court.

The truth is, work settings for attorneys vary widely. Lawyers work in their own offices and those of colleagues, in conference rooms, in law libraries, and in other locations. Generally, such locations are quite comfortable, with all the trappings one would expect of modern offices. For those who are just getting started or who work for nonprofit organizations, though, office settings may be quite modest—small, cramped, and simply appointed. At the other extreme, senior partners or attorneys holding high-level corporate positions may enjoy large, luxurious offices.

Outside of law offices and court facilities, lawyers may perform a variety of fieldwork, depending on job assignments and the nature of the work in their specialty. For example, an attorney may spend hours sitting in a dusty, poorly lit basement of a government building, poring through old documents. An attorney preparing for a lawsuit may visit the hospital room of an accident victim and the site where an automobile crash occurred. Another may fly to another city to take a deposition or interview a potential witness.

Perhaps the most important factor in working conditions for attorneys is not location, but time. Many lawyers put in very long hours. This is especially common for attorneys who are just starting their careers. A young lawyer employed by a large law firm may be expected to work sixty hours a week or more. Senior lawyers may also work long hours, although some enjoy more favorable schedules than beginning attorneys. Working hours may vary for lawyers employed by government agencies or nonprofit organizations. In some cases, a forty-hour workweek is the norm.

Strategies for Finding the Jobs

Law can be a highly rewarding field. So it's no surprise that it is also a competitive one. Those who want to practice law not only face stiff competition in getting admitted to law school, but also can encounter difficulty in landing good jobs.

According to the U.S. Department of Education, over 680,000 lawyers are employed in the United States. When the numbers of those graduating from law school each year are added to the large number of attorneys already practicing law, the job market can be tight.

This doesn't mean those considering law should give up their hopes. But anyone determined to become an attorney should be aware of this situation and be willing to work diligently in the job search process.

A primary method of finding jobs in this field is to use the processes established by universities to help their graduates find jobs. These processes vary from one school to another, but virtually all law schools consider helping graduates find jobs to be one of their responsibilities, and provide services accordingly. Typical assistance includes the following:

- Job fairs where prospective employers visit a college campus and interview students who will be graduating during that academic year
- Help in scheduling on-campus interviews on an individualized basis
- Assistance in scheduling off-campus interviews
- Correspondence with prospective employers and posting of job openings on bulletin boards, Web pages, and other sites
- Development of recruitment handbooks that profile prospective graduates
- Publication of lists of job openings
- Individualized counseling and advisement regarding the career search process

At the Vanderbilt University Law School, for example, an on-campus recruitment program is held every year during the fall semester. Representatives from more than 500 offices take part, representing more than thirty states. Both second-year and third-year students participate. Students in their first year are also assisted in finding summer employment.

In addition, prospective law school graduates can conduct their own job searches using a variety of resources. This might include singling out prospective employers and sending them introductory letters with résumés, using personal contacts of friends and family, and consulting publications that list job openings for attorneys.

A number of companies offer free or fee-based information about job opportunities. For example, the FindLaw Career Center at careers.findlaw.com provides listings of job openings in the legal industry, links to job search directories, a featured legal job for the day, and other helpful information. Another useful website is the "law jobs" section of law.com (lawjobs.com). It offers listings of current job openings for attorneys along with information from legal recruiters and other sources.

Related Occupations

Persons who hold law degrees don't necessarily practice law. They may go on to take other related positions such as judgeships. Or they may work for corporations, write about law-related matters, or perform other functions.

In addition, a number of other occupations carry related responsibilities. Many related positions do not require law degrees but may be of interest to those who have studied political science.

Judges

While in college, you may have sat in class and thought that someday you'd like to take on the role of professor (if so, be sure to look at options outlined in the chapter on teaching). For lawyers, a similar line of thought is to aspire to become a judge.

Some lawyers do move on to hold positions as judges. Although the number of judges is relatively small compared to the number of attorneys, this is a reasonable goal for those who become attorneys and have the right combination of drive and intelligence.

Types of judges include the following:

- Administrative law judges
- Appellate court judges
- County court judges
- General trial court judges
- Magistrates
- Municipal court judges

Professional Associations for Attorneys and Related Professionals

American Bar
    Association
750 N. Lake Shore Dr.
Chicago, IL 60611
abanet.org
Members/Purpose: Serves more than 400,000 attorneys, law students, and
    others interested in the legal profession. The organization includes
    twenty-two sections and more than eighty commissions.

Training: Sponsors conferences and seminars; provides educational materials.

Journals/Publications: Publishes *ABA Journal* as well as a variety of other publications, including those focusing on the practice of law in specific areas such as *Journal of Affordable Housing and Community Development, Antitrust Law Journal, Family Law Quarterly, The Labor Lawyer, Procurement Lawyer, The Urban Lawyer*, and more.

Job Listings: Offers job information to students and online links to employment sites.

Association of American
Law Schools
1201 Connecticut Ave. NW, Suite 800
Washington, DC 20036-2605
aals.org

Members/Purpose: Works to improve the legal profession through legal education; serves as the learned society for law teachers.

Training: Annual meeting plus five to six conferences a year.

Journal/Publications: *Journal of Legal Education*; quarterly newsletter; directory of law teachers.

The Canadian
Bar Association
902-50 O'Connor St.
Ottawa, ON
Canada K1P 6L2
cba.org

Members/Purpose: Serves attorneys and law students.

Training: Sponsors conferences.

Federal Bar Association
221 M St. NW
Washington, DC 20006
fedbar.org

Members/Purpose: Members include 15,000 attorneys, judges, legislators, and others; supports continuing education and community service.

Training: Holds annual meeting.

Journal/Publication: *The Federal Lawyer* magazine; FBA publications catalog; electronic jobs board.

Law School Admission Council
Law Services
661 Penn St.
Newtown, PA 18940
lsac.org
Members/Purpose: Nonprofit organization whose members are 200 law schools in the United States and Canada; administers the Law School Admission Test (LSAT); offers a wealth of information at its website, including sample tests and a searchable guide to accredited law schools.

9

Path 4:
Nonprofit Management

The typical political science major may look forward to a future career in government, law, or teaching. But another area of potential employment is often overlooked: working as a manager or other professional in a nonprofit organization. In fact, nonprofit organizations represent a huge area of employment.

You may have noticed a list of professional organizations at the end of each of the preceding three chapters. These groups can be helpful in a variety of ways. But did it occur to you that they themselves represent employment potential? Virtually every professional association employs a staff of managers and other employees.

Actually, the term *nonprofit* is somewhat misleading because it is so often connected with volunteerism and is largely separated from the "business" world. But nonprofit activities are in fact big business. Making money may not be the main goal of such organizations, but in other respects they operate very much like businesses. This includes maintaining a staff of paid employees whose jobs are to carry out the work of the organization. For example, the American Society of Association Executives employs a president and an executive vice president to manage its affairs. The organization also employs a full-time staff of more than 100 persons.

Other organizations have similar stories. Some have only a few staff members, while others provide employment for scores of workers. Some have objectives related to the political process, government, or related matters. To work for them, having a political science background can be especially helpful. For countless other organizations, a college degree in any liberal arts field, including political science, can provide the background for an entry-level position—with additional job experience, even a variety of positions, including top-level executive management.

Definition of the Career Path

Serving in nonprofit management can take a variety of forms. Some jobs consist of providing overall administrative duties. A common job title in the nonprofit sector is executive director, with the president being a member of the board that oversees the group rather than being an employee. In this structure, the executive director is the highest ranking paid employee. Related positions include titles such as associate executive director and assistant director.

In some organizations, a business-type structure is used with the top paid position being that of president. Related positions include vice president, associate vice president, and assistant vice president. Often a voluntary board of directors provides oversight, headed by a chairperson.

Other commonly found positions include titles such as director and coordinator. Examples include director of member services and public information coordinator.

Possible Job Titles

Following are some representative job titles in nonprofit organizations:

- Assistant to the president or vice president
- Associate executive director or vice president
- Chief operating officer
- Development associate, director, or officer
- Direct marketing coordinator
- Director of affiliate services, communications, education, finance and administration, or public affairs
- Executive administrator or director
- Field director
- Major gift officer
- Media relations director
- Planned giving specialist
- President
- Program associate, director, or officer
- Public relations coordinator
- Regional development manager
- Senior consultant
- Senior grants administrator

- Senior program officer
- Vice president for development
- Volunteer coordinator

Possible Employers

Where does employment in the nonprofit sector lead? A career in this area may mean working for a private foundation, a professional organization, an interest group, a charity, or one of many other organizations.

Foundations

How would you like to have a job where a major duty is giving away money? That's the situation for many managers who work for private foundations. These nonprofit organizations exist to hold and manage funds that have been donated by wealthy individuals, families, corporations, and others. In most cases, this also involves giving away funds in the form of grants. In fact, some kinds of foundations are required by law to give away at least 5 percent of their investment assets each year.

Thousands of private and corporate foundations exist in the United States and Canada. Some are small, obscure entities unknown except to the few recipients of their grants and the bank officers or others who manage them. Others, such as the Ford Foundation and the Kellogg Foundation, are huge enterprises holding billions of dollars in assets and employing hundreds of people.

The Philadelphia Foundation is an example of a community foundation, an organization that serves the needs of specific cities or communities. This foundation has over $100 million in assets and distributes millions of dollars each year in grants to nonprofit groups in southeastern Pennsylvania. Recipients of grants may include neighborhood revitalization groups, human service programs, schools and education projects, health care initiatives, and other groups.

According to a survey conducted by the Columbus Foundation of Columbus, Ohio, community foundations receive more than $2 billion each year in donations. Over twenty such groups have more than $200 million in assets each, and more than forty hold assets in excess of $100 million. As these foundations continue to grow and others are formed, job opportunities are expanding for those interested in nonprofit management.

Another type of foundation is the family foundation, where the members of a family have set up an organization to honor family members and dispense funds, typically to meet local needs or support a special interest area. These can be found in almost every city and even in some small towns or rural areas.

A number of companies have established corporate foundations where a portion of profits is used to make donations for purposes consistent with the company's objectives or philosophy. For instance, the McDonald's Foundation supports the needs of children through a variety of grant programs.

The following are some major foundations:

Foundation	Location
Abell Foundation	Baltimore, Maryland
Annenberg Foundation	St. David's, Pennsylvania
Carnegie Corporation	New York, New York
Danforth Foundation	St. Louis, Missouri
Ford Foundation	New York, New York
Heinz Endowments	Pittsburgh, Pennsylvania
Robert Wood Johnson Foundation	Princeton, New Jersey
W. M. Keck Foundation	Los Angeles, California
W. K. Kellogg Foundation	Troy, Michigan
Lilly Endowment	Indianapolis, Indiana
John D. and Catherine T. MacArthur Foundation	Chicago, Illinois
Pew Charitable Trusts	Philadelphia, Pennsylvania
Rockefeller Foundation	New York, New York

Associations

A great American tradition is the state, regional, or national association that brings together people with common interests, which often are occupations. For example, associations listed at the end of each of the preceding three chapters are based on occupational interests.

Examples of associations include the following:

- Alabama Textile Manufacturers Association
- Alaska Bar Association
- American Business Women's Association
- American Payroll Association
- California Automotive Wholesalers' Association

- Florida Recreation and Park Association
- Hawaii Credit Union League
- Home Care Association of New York State
- Oklahoma Municipal League
- Self Storage Association

Interest Groups

Want to save the whales? Stop child abuse? Promote the use of atomic energy? Eliminate abortion? Expand the availability of abortion? Whatever your interest, chances are at least one special interest group can bring you together with others of the same interest and agenda. Like other nonprofit organizations, interest groups typically employ staff to coordinate their affairs. Examples of interest groups include the following:

- Center for Advancement of Public Policy
- Center for Law and Social Policy
- Center for Responsive Politics
- Children's Defense Fund
- Committee to Protect Journalists
- Dispute Resolution Center
- Domestic Violence Program
- Economic Policy Institute
- Environmental Defense Fund
- Family Resource Coalition
- Fund for Peace
- Hispanic Community Talent Inventory
- National Center for Family Literacy
- National Center for Strategic Nonprofit Planning and Community Leadership
- National Rifle Association
- Partners in Parenting
- Public Employees Roundtable
- Sierra Club
- Women's Information Network Against Breast Cancer

Charities

Many organizations exist specifically to raise funds for needy causes. They are not necessarily a completely separate category from interest groups or other organizations, but their emphasis usually is to collect funds for redistribution to groups or individuals who need assistance or to fund research or other efforts aimed at helping those in need. Examples of charities include the following:

- American Heart Association
- American Lung Association
- Big Brothers/Big Sisters
- Family Abuse Services
- Habitat for Humanity
- Legal Aid Service
- Neighborhood Justice Center
- Parent Assistance League
- Salvation Army
- Student Rural Health Coalition

Sample Job Announcement

The following job opening was advertised by the Alzheimer's Association. Although this particular opening required several years of job experience, it is typical of the kinds of jobs a political science graduate may qualify for in the nonprofit sector.

OPENING: POLICY ANALYST

The Alzheimer's Association, a national voluntary health agency with a strong grassroots chapter network, seeks an experienced policy analyst/advocate in its Washington, D.C., office to lead and direct its state health and long-term care policy work nationwide. The analyst manages the Association's award-winning state policy clearinghouse, coordinates strategic policy analysis, and develops collaborations with national organizations of state officials.

Specific job functions include the following:

- Develop Association positions, strategies, model legislation, and supporting materials on priority issues, and promote their effective use by chapter advocates in the states.
- Monitor state policy developments to identify health issues and opportunities for advocacy.
- Facilitate regular exchange of information and strategies on state issues among health advocates in the chapter network.
- Publish a bimonthly *State Policy Report* on health issues for state advocates and public officials.

---

continued

- Develop collaborations with national organizations of state officials, including conferences, workshops, and policy reports, to further the Association's state policy objectives.

Successful candidates will have a degree in political science, health policy, or a related field; 3–5 years' experience in state legislative or health policy; and proven success in coordinating advocacy efforts.

The position also requires experience in managing computerized databases to maintain a clearinghouse of advocacy issues for the Association's 150 chapters nationwide.

The Toughest Job You Ever Loved?

If you want to work hard, earn very little money, but gain invaluable experience, consider joining the Peace Corps. Certainly this avenue isn't for everyone, but it can be a great experience for political science graduates who want to serve others while gaining some valuable life experience.

For more information about the Peace Corps, contact its national headquarters at

**The Paul D. Coverdell
Peace Corps Headquarters**
111 20th St. NW
Washington, DC 20526
peacecorps.gov

AmeriCorps

While the Peace Corps may be the most famous service outreach program, it is by no means the only one. You can gain similar experiences without working in a third-world country. A domestic program of potential interest to political science majors seeking to broaden their experience is AmeriCorps. This national service program places participants in community-based positions. Some participants join before attending college, others participate after completing their degrees, and some use the program as a break from college. Service projects range from working in schools to rebuilding homes damaged by floods or hurricanes. In exchange for a year of service, AmeriCorps volunteers receive a living stipend, health insurance, and an education voucher that can be used to pay back student loans or for tuition for additional college studies. For more information, contact

AmeriCorps
Corporation for National and Community Service
1201 New York Ave. NW
Washington, DC 20525
nationalservice.org

Training and Qualifications

In many cases, general preparation in political science provides the necessary background for entry-level jobs in nonprofit management. In addition, some schools offer courses that specifically address issues related to nonprofit administration. These may be offered within a political science department. They may also be offered through a school of business, where students from other disciplines, including political science, are welcome to participate.

For example, Washington University of St. Louis offers a 15-credit Advanced Certificate in Non-Profit Management. The program covers topics such as leading and managing nonprofit organizations, interacting with boards of directors, supervising volunteers and professionals, raising funds, marketing, evaluating programs, and financial management. For more information, contact

Non-Profit Management Program
University College, Campus Box 1085
Washington University
1 Brookings Dr.
St. Louis, MO 63130-4899
wustl.edu

Another program worth noting is offered by New School University through its Robert J. Milano School of Management and Urban Policy. This college offers a master of science degree in nonprofit management. The New School is located in New York City where, according to school officials, one in seven people works in the nonprofit sector. For information, write to

MS Program in Nonprofit Management
Milano Graduate School
New School University
66 W. 12th St.
New York, NY 10011
newschool.edu

Even if you gain an entry-level position, you'll find that working in the nonprofit sector often requires special knowledge, gained either in college, on the job, or through a combination of the two. Here are some common topics covered by managers in nonprofit settings:

- Annual fund strategies
- Basic fund-raising principles
- Basic grantsmanship
- Building endowments
- Corporate and foundation fund-raising
- Direct mail fund-raising
- Effective proposal development
- Ethics of fund-raising
- Grant-writing basics
- Managing volunteers
- Office management techniques
- Organizing capital campaigns
- Planned-giving programs
- Principles of grant management
- Public relations strategies
- Strategic planning
- Using computers in fund-raising
- Working with boards
- Writing for development

Fortunately, many of these skills are consistent with the kind of knowledge and interest levels typically demonstrated by political science students and graduates. With additional training and job experience, the typical political science major can readily adapt to the work that is performed in nonprofit organizations.

Earnings

Salaries paid by nonprofit organizations vary enormously. For a small community agency, salaries may lag far behind those of private businesses. For a large national organization, salaries may be quite good, especially for upper-level managers.

On average, salaries earned in the nonprofit sector are not as high as those for comparable positions in private business. Certainly, such benefits as stock options and profit-sharing plans are not available in the nonprofit world. And since the dominant purpose is performing some type of service, the culture of most nonprofit organizations runs counter to the profit-making mentality of businesses.

Still, salaries for managers in nonprofit groups can be attractive. In addition, fringe benefits can be appealing, and attractive features such as deferred compensation are becoming more common.

The *NonProfit Times* conducts an annual survey of salaries of subscribers. In a survey published in 2002, it found anticipated salary averages for executives in nonprofit organizations as follows:

Chief executive officer	$90,903
Chief financial officer	$61,518
Program director	$53,782
Planned gifts officer	$58,753
Development director	$57,312
Major gifts officer	$62,951
Chief of direct marketing	$53,011
Director of volunteers	$35,349

The *NonProfit Times* notes that salaries vary widely not only by type of organization, but also by size. Chief executives in organizations with annual budgets of more than $10 million, for example, earn average salaries of more than $100,000.

Results of surveys conducted by the American Society of Association Executives (ASAE) have found that the size of the organization is a major factor. The ASAE found that the median salary for CEOs of associations with budgets under $300,000 was $53,000, while the median salary for CEOs of associations with budgets over $15 million was $289,134. Salary averages tend to fall between these two extremes for associations among neither the smallest nor the largest of their type. ASAE surveys have found that a number of other factors also affect salary levels, such as size of staff, association income, geographic area, and experience on the job.

Working Conditions

Working conditions in nonprofit management vary widely. Typically, standard office settings can be expected. Surroundings might range from a cubicle with a desk and phone to a large, more attractive office. The smaller the organization or the less experienced the worker, the more likely the work setting will be simple.

Aside from the basics of office locations and furnishings, one common advantage of the nonprofit setting is the flexibility in when and how work may be performed. For example, employers may allow some degree of "telecommuting," where staff members work out of their homes instead of reporting to an office. Flextime, where workers are expected to work a minimum number of hours but may adjust schedules according to their own personal preferences, is also offered by some employers.

Work settings may also vary if travel or casework is required. For instance, a program officer for a foundation may travel to locations where grants have been awarded and review the progress made possible through grant funding. For a community foundation, this might mean driving across town and visiting a shelter for the homeless. For a program officer with the Ford Foundation, it could mean flying to Colombia to review progress in establishing a preschool program for disadvantaged children.

Strategies for Finding the Jobs

There is no single method for finding jobs in the nonprofit sector. One place to start is your college's career placement office. Be alert for campus visitations by representatives of nonprofit organizations, as well as for postings of job openings with such groups. Then apply for any that interest you.

The classified sections of major newspapers include ads for jobs with nonprofit organizations. Newspapers published in smaller cities will include ads for local job openings, but you'll need to consult major papers such as the *New York Times* and *Washington Post* for regional or national openings.

You can also contact organizations directly and request information on job openings and how you might apply. Many organizations now include such information online; you need only check out their websites.

Perhaps the best sources of job information are publications targeted specifically to those who are already employed in the nonprofit sector or who have other direct ties such as service on boards of directors. For example, the *Chronicle of Philanthropy*, published twenty-four times a year, includes an exhaustive list of job openings in nonprofit organizations in each issue. In addition, the *Chronicle* is a solid source of information about events and trends in the nonprofit world. It covers fund-raising ideas and techniques, reports on tax and court rulings, and provides information about conferences and other professional development opportunities, among other topics. For more information, contact

Chronicle of Philanthropy
1255 23rd St. NW
Washington, DC 20037
philanthropy.com

While the *Chronicle of Philanthropy* focuses on private giving, a more general publication is the *NonProfit Times*. This newspaper bills itself as "The Leading Business Publication for Nonprofit Management." Along with news of interest to those working in nonprofit organizations, each issue includes a number of job openings. For information, contact

NonProfit Times
120 Littleton Rd., Suite 120
Parsippany, NJ 07054
nptimes.com

An online job service you may want to check out is

The Community Career Center
Enterprise, Inc.
2160 W. Charleston
Las Vegas, NV 89102
nonprofitjobs.org

The Association of Fundraising Professionals (formerly the National Society of Fund Raising Executives) is a good source of information about the fund-raising profession. This progressive organization has more than 26,000 members in chapters located throughout North America. Members hold a variety of jobs in nonprofit and charitable organizations.

An especially noteworthy service of this association is its certification programs. Through its Certified Fundraising Executive (CFRE) and Advanced Certified Fundraising Executive (ACFRE) programs, the association provides certification that professionals have met certain standards for excellence in fund-raising. A person can use these credentials to enhance other educational backgrounds after having established some experience in the field. The person with a political science background who has a CFRE designation may fare better in advancing on the job or seeking a new job than the one who doesn't have the CFRE designation.

The Association of Fundraising Professionals also provides a variety of educational opportunities. Among these are the annual International Conference on Fundraising, the Executive Leadership Institute, the Survey Course on Fundraising, and the First Course in Fundraising. For more information about this organization, contact

Association of Fundraising Professionals
1101 King St., Suite 700
Alexandria, VA 22314
afpnet.org

Related Occupations

Many of the skills involved in nonprofit management can be applied in other career areas. Skills such as planning, organizing, communicating, and supervising others can be applied in small businesses, large corporations, and other settings. Some representative job titles for related career areas follow:

- Account executive
- Director, quality assurance
- Hospital administrator
- Human resource manager
- Labor relations supervisor
- Management consultant
- Marketing director
- Office manager
- Sales manager
- Teacher
- Technical editor

Professional Associations for Nonprofit Executives, Managers, and Related Professionals

**American Society of
    Association Executives**
1575 I St. NW
Washington, DC 20005
asaenet.org

Members/Purpose: Promotes and supports excellence and professionalism among executives of trade associations, individual membership societies, voluntary organizations, and other nonprofit associations.

Training: Annual conference as well as special conferences and symposia.

Journal/Publications: *Association Management* magazine; newsletters.

Association of Fundraising Professionals

1101 King St., Suite 700
Alexandria, VA 22314
afpnet.org

Members/Purpose: Serves individuals responsible for generating philanthropic support for a variety of nonprofit, charitable organizations.

Training: Annual conference, courses on fund-raising, certification program.

Journal/Publication: Quarterly journal, *Advancing Philanthropy*; newsletters.

National Council of Nonprofit Associations

1030 15 St., NW, Suite 870
Washington, DC 20005

Members/Purpose: Coordinating group for thirty nonprofit organizations. Provides information, advocacy, and professional development opportunities.

Training: Annual conference and biennial regional membership meetings.

Publications: Various publications on taxation, organizing associations, and other topics.

Additional Resources

Books

Butterworth, Amy S., and Sally A. Migliore, eds. *National Directory of Internships.* Springfield, Va.: National Society for Experiential Education, 1989.

Camenson, Blythe. *Careers for Legal Eagles and Other Law-and-Order Types.* Lincolnwood, Ill.: VGM Career Books, 1998.

Carroll's County Directory 2002. Bethesda, Md.: Carroll Publishing Co., 2002.

Carroll's Federal Directory 2002. Bethesda, Md.: Carroll Publishing Co., 2002.

Carroll's State Directory 2002: Executive, Legislative, Judicial. Bethesda, Md.: Carroll Publishing Co., 2002.

The College Board Index of Majors and Graduate Degrees 2003. New York: College Board, 2002.

Colvin, Donna, et al., eds. *Good Works: A Guide to Careers in Social Change.* Fort Lee, N.J.: Barricade Books, 1994.

Curzan, M. H., ed. *Careers and the Study of Political Science: A Guide for Undergraduates.* Washington, D.C.: American Political Science Association, 1994.

Directory of City Policy Officials & Resource Guide 2002. Washington, D.C.: National League of Cities, 2002.

Edelfelt, Roy. *Careers in Education.* Lincolnwood, Ill.: VGM Career Books, 1997.

Editors of VGM Career Books. *Careers Encyclopedia.* Lincolnwood, Ill.: VGM Career Books, 2001.

137

Editors of VGM Career Books. *Resumes for Government Careers.* Lincoln-wood, Ill.: VGM Career Books, 1996.

King, Richard. *From Making a Profit to Making a Difference: How to Launch Your New Career in Nonprofits.* River Forest, Ill.: Planning Communications, 2000.

Krannich, Ronald L. *The Complete Guide to Public Employment.* Manassas Park, Va.: Impact Publications, 1994.

Mantis, Hillary. *Alternative Careers for Lawyers.* New York: Princeton Review, 1997.

Moody, Wayne, et al., eds. *Patterson's American Education 2002.* Schaumburg, Ill.: Educational Directories Inc., 2002.

The Municipal Year Book 2002: The Authoritative Source Book of Local Government Data and Developments. Washington, D.C.: International City/County Management Association, 2002.

National Standards for Civics and Government. Calabaras, Calif.: Center for Civic Education, 1994.

Newman, Joseph W. *America's Teachers: An Introduction to Education.* Boston: Allyn & Bacon, 2001.

Quain, Anthony. *The Political Reference Almanac 2001–2002.* Arlington, Va.: Polisci Books, 2001.

Rowh, Mark et al. *Careers in Government.* Lincolnwood, Ill.: VGM Career Books, 2001.

Rowh, Mark, et al. *Opportunities in Government Careers.* Lincolnwood, Ill.: VGM Career Books, 2001.

U.S. Department of Labor. *Occupational Outlook Handbook 2002–2003.* Chicago: VGM Career Books, 2002.

Wehnes, Lynn Bracken. *The Harvard College Guide to Careers in Government and Politics.* Cambridge, Mass.: Harvard University, 1992.

Yerema, Richard. *Canada's Top 100 Employers.* Toronto: Mediacorp Canada Inc., 2003.

Journals

ABA Journal
abanet.org/journal/home.html

American Journal of Political Science
jstor.org/journals/00925853.html

American Political Science Review
apsa.com

American Politics Quarterly
sagepub.co.uk/journals/details/j0091.html

Association Management
asaenet.org/magazine

Campaigns and Elections
campaignline.com

Canadian Journal of
Political Science
wlu.ca/~wwwpress/jrls/cjps/english/cjps.html

Common Cause Magazine
commoncause.org

Equal Opportunity
eop.com

Foreign Service Journal
afsa.org

Government Executive
govexec.com

Independent School
nais.org

Instructor Magazine
teacher.scholastic.com/products/instructor.htm

The Journal of Comparative Politics
http://web.gc.cuny.edu/jcp

Lawyers Weekly USA
lawyersweeklyusa.com

Legislative Studies Quarterly
uiowa.edu/~lsq

National Law Journal
nlj.com

Philanthropic Digest
P.O. Box 325
Clinton, NY 13323

Philanthropy Journal
philanthropyjournal.com

Policy Studies Journal
siu.edu/~psj

Political Science Quarterly
psqonline.org

PS: Political Science and Politics
apsanet.org/PS

Public Administration Review
aspanet.org/publications/par/index2.html

Public Affairs Report
igs.berkeley.edu/publications/par

Public Opinion Quarterly
journals.uchicago.edu/POQ/home.html

State and Local Government Review
cviog.uga.edu/slgr

Student Lawyer
abanet.org/lsd/stulawyer

Women and Politics
american.edu/oconnor/wandp/journal/journal.html

Other Resources

American Association for Employment in Education
aaee.org

American Planning Association
planning.org

American Political Science Association
apsanet.org

American Society for Public Administration
aspanet.org

Careers in Government (Web-based employment information)
careersingovernment.com

Chicago Tribune
chicagotribune.com

Chronicle of Higher Education
chronicle.com

Los Angeles Times
latimes.com

National Association of Schools of Public Affairs and Administration
naspaa.org

New York Times
nytimes.com

NonProfit Times
nptimes.com

Washington Post
washingtonpost.com

Index